WOMEN WHO RISK

"The stories in this book have broken my heart, put tears on my face, and pressed me to my knees in prayer for women who have risked everything to follow Jesus. Their steadfast faith when facing death, their strength to endure abuse, their courage to bear witness of the Truth, and their sheer joy in Jesus make them women to emulate. Read this, and you will love Jesus more and be filled with gratitude that He loves you, and me, and women everywhere. Thank you, Tom and JoAnn Doyle, for these incredible, jaw-dropping stories."

—ANNE GRAHAM LOTZ, AUTHOR, *JESUS IN ME*

"Eye-opening, awe-inspiring, praise-evoking—*Women Who Risk* is an exhilarating peek behind the veil to see how, despite the danger, Jesus is reaching and empowering Muslim women to live for him. Let our friends, Tom and JoAnn, take you on an exhilarating journey of discovery that will enrich your faith and encourage your soul. You'll be riveted and enthralled by these astounding stories!"

—LEE AND LESLIE STROBEL, AUTHORS,
SPIRITUAL MISMATCH AND *THE CASE FOR CHRIST*

"Like war correspondents, Tom and JoAnn Doyle report from behind enemy lines about the spiritual combat conditions we, who live under a Declaration of Independence, cannot comprehend. *Women Who Risk* is not fiction. These are all real-life stories that have been lived out in the midst of savage brutality and unmitigated evil. There is a higher battle than the ones played out in the Middle East today. It's a battle for human souls. Here is wrenching fear and pain transformed to ecstatic joy, a gritty, compelling account of our world God calls us Christians to confront with His transforming power."

—JEANNE HENDRICKS, SPEAKER, AUTHOR, AND
WIFE OF THE LATE DR. HOWARD HENDRICKS

"*Women Who Risk* revolves around two incredible truths. The first is the power of Jesus to change the hearts and lives of women and their families in the Muslim world. And the second is the amazing way God has used Tom and JoAnn Doyle to introduce us to these modern-day heroes of the faith. Grab a cup of *qahwa* (Turkish coffee) or *shay* (Turkish tea) and sit down to read these amazing stories of Muslim women who have come to know, follow, and proclaim Jesus. But be sure to grab a large mug and choose a comfortable chair because you won't be able to stop reading once you begin."

—CHARLES DYER, PROFESSOR AT LARGE, MOODY
BIBLE INSTITUTE, AND RADIO HOST, *THE LAND
AND THE BOOK*; AND KATHY DYER

"This book is a powerful portrait of spiritual heroism. Tom and JoAnn Doyle have woven together incredibly impacting true stories of women in the Middle East, women whose courageous walk of faith is a testament to the resurrection power of the Savior who has changed their lives. It also illustrates profoundly how Christ cares about women, and cares infinitely."

—CRAIG PARSHALL, *NEW YORK TIMES* BESTSELLING
AUTHOR AND SENIOR VICE PRESIDENT, NATIONAL
RELIGIOUS BROADCASTERS; AND JANET PARSHALL,
RADIO HOST, NATIONALLY SYNDICATED *IN THE MARKET*

"For many years we have read books aloud together in the evenings. Among the very best and most edifying have been the works of Tom Doyle. But with the release of *Women Who Risk*, Tom, now joined by JoAnn, have outdone themselves. The book reads like an adventure novel—fast-paced, intriguing, spiritually edifying, and faith building. We couldn't put it down."

—J. P. MORELAND, DISTINGUISHED PROFESSOR
OF PHILOSOPHY, TALBOT SCHOOL OF THEOLOGY,
BIOLA UNIVERSITY; AND HOPE MORELAND

"No couple has inspired us more than Tom and JoAnn Doyle as they fearlessly and faithfully walk side-by-side into the darkest places on earth. All to share Christ with those who desperately need to hear it and in places no one else has dared to go. Their riveting stories will open your eyes to the pain and ignite your passion to join Christ in His mighty work of saving, healing, and loving the Muslim world."

—JASON ELAM, SPECIAL AMBASSADOR, BIBLE
TRANSLATION, SEED COMPANY, AND FORMER NFL
KICKER; AND TAMY ELAM, ADVOCATE, SEED COMPANY

"*Women Who Risk* is an inspiring, challenging peek inside the real world of some of Tom and JoAnn's friends who know "the cost of discipleship" very few of us in America will ever have to consider. This book will change the way you think about giving your life away and lead you to be willing to pay a greater price in following Jesus regardless of the cost!"

—TODD PETERSON, FORMER NFL KICKER; CHAIRMAN,
PRO ATHLETES OUTREACH; CHAIRMAN EMERITUS, SEED
COMPANY; AND BOARD MEMBER, PASSION CITY CHURCH;
AND SUSAN PETERSON, FOUNDER AND CEO, RELISH AND
CABELL'S DESIGNS, AND BOARD TRUSTEE, YOUNG LIFE

"Tom and JoAnn Doyle are courageous, Holy Spirit–filled Christians with a willingness to brave dangerous circumstances, risk personal safety, and lay down their lives for those to whom they minister. I deeply appreciate their dedication to both Muslims and the Jewish people, bringing them the message of God's love through Jesus the Messiah. This book will advance your understanding and prayer burden for some of the most marginalized and imperiled believers in the world."

—MITCH GLASER, PRESIDENT, CHOSEN PEOPLE
MINISTRIES; AND ZHAVA GLASER

"I love the stories in this book—many of which brought tears to my eyes—as they are snapshots of what God is doing among the Muslim women in the Middle East today. Jesus is pouring His special grace on Muslim women because He came to set the captives free, and in Islam, it is the women who are oppressed and treated as slaves. The greatest weapon we have against the dark spirit of Islam is love."

—HORMOZ SHARIAT, PRESIDENT, IRAN ALIVE
MINISTRIES; AND DONNELL SHARIAT

"Tom and JoAnn are a dynamic team in every way! Their love and passion for Jesus and for each other overflow into every life whom God places in their path. You, too, will be touched as you read the engaging stories of real-life women who are also bringing Christ's light into the dark world of Islam."

—MIKE AND CHERI FITZSIMMONS, FOUNDERS,
MORNINGSTAR TRANSFORMATIONAL TOURS

"As mentors and friends, no one has shown us more about how to love our Muslim neighbors than Tom and JoAnn Doyle. The true stories captured in these pages will inspire your faith and awaken your heart to the powerful move of God happening among women in the Middle East. Make no mistake, the church is alive and unstoppable!"

—BRYSON VOGELTANZ, PRESIDENT AND CEO, PARTNERS
INTERNATIONAL; AND EMILY VOGELTANZ

"Heartbreaking and inspiring, *Women Who Risk* unveils the incredible stories that are currently happening in the Muslim world. Women are meeting Jesus in unprecedented numbers and in supernatural ways. *Warning*: This book is a page-turner that will grip your heart and blow your mind. It reads like the Acts of the Apostles. God is great!"

—JIM TOMBERLIN, AUTHOR; MERGER SPECIALIST,
THE UNSTUCK GROUP; AND CHIEF OF STAFF, CHRIST
FELLOWSHIP, MIAMI, FLORIDA; AND DERYL TOMBERLIN

"*Women Who Risk* is your chance to walk through some of the world's most challenging places with JoAnn and Tom Doyle. Their riveting accounts are of bold women whom Jesus has met through their dreams, visions, and miracles. This book is a powerful read that will stretch your faith and inspire you to live with courage for the kingdom."
  —BOB SHANK, FOUNDER AND CEO, THE MASTER'S
  PROGRAM; AND CHERI SHANK, SPECIAL EVENTS AND
  WOMEN'S PROGRAM, THE MASTER'S PROGRAM

"Disillusioned with flat Christianity? Wondering if God still does miracles? Afraid your life can't make an impact? Then this is the book for you. *Women Who Risk* is a peek behind the veil to the personal battles and miraculous movements of the spiritual warriors of our day. These new Jesus followers, and their real-life stories of vulnerability, faith, challenge, and courage, will not only inspire your own spiritual journey but also help you see the God who sees you."
  —KADI COLE, LEADERSHIP CONSULTANT, EXECUTIVE
  COACH, AND AUTHOR, *DEVELOPING FEMALE LEADERS*

"Jesus is rescuing women in the Muslim world! Their beautifully told stories will encourage your own faith and leave you in awe at the Savior who is unwilling that any—including those shackled in the bondage of Islam—should perish (2 Pet. 3:9)."
  —TODD NETTLETON, RADIO HOST, *THE VOICE OF
  THE MARTYRS*; AND CHARLOTTE NETTLETON,
  WESLEYAN CHRISTIAN SCHOOL

"We were captivated from the very first page with the identification of these women as *Secret Agents for Jesus in the Muslim World*. The miracle of their heart healing, the powerful testimony of how they daily bear witness of Jesus' love by word and deed in a dangerous world, confronts us to live beyond our religion. We need to see and hear and reach out as they do, with Jesus' heart."
  —RAY BENTLEY, PASTOR, MARANATHA
  CHAPEL; AND VICKI BENTLEY

"*Women Who Risk* reads like pages from a modern-day book of Acts, with twists and turns at every corner. The testimonies grab the heart, fascinate our faith, and challenge the very core of our Christianity. These stories are crucial for this hour in history, a time of global unrest and uncertainty. These sisters and brothers are models of the saints who depend on the trustworthy lordship of Jesus, His love, God's supernatural power, and miracles. God will use this book to transform your life, turning your heart to repentance, gratitude, and compassion."

—JOSHUA LINGEL, PRESIDENT, MISSION MUSLIM WORLD
    UNIVERSITY AND i2 MINISTRIES; AND SARA LINGEL

"Tom and JoAnn not only have the pulse of the Middle East; they care deeply for women. How might we see a movement of God through war and famine? Through *Women Who Risk*!"

—JEFF GERHARDT, CEO, CENTIX LIFE TECHNOLOGIES,
    AND BOARD CHAIRMAN, UNCHARTED MINISTRIES;
    AND HEATHER GERHARDT, WORSHIP LEADER AND
    CONTENT CREATOR, YOUTUBE CHANNEL

"My heart was gripped to read the stories of women in the Middle East who, facing desperate situations, are utterly transformed by Jesus. If it can happen to them, then there is hope for any relationship here! Open these pages and enter a world where God's power is on display in astounding ways!"

—BRUCE PEPPIN, AUTHOR, *THE BEST IS YET TO BE*, AND
    SPEAKER, FINISHING LIFE WELL; AND KATHLEEN PEPPIN

"We are living in a world full of injustices. One of the greatest being the plight of Muslim women. Tom and JoAnn not only have given a look into that world but also have revealed how God is powerfully penetrating what has been closed—setting Muslim women free to share and demonstrate God's love to those around them. Indeed, God is at work in miraculous ways!"

—DAVID ECKLEBARGER, FORMER PRESIDENT AND CEO, SPANISH
    HOUSE MINISTRIES/UNILIT; AND CATHY ECKLEBARGER

WOMEN
WHO RISK

WOMEN
WHO RISK

SECRET AGENTS FOR JESUS
IN THE MUSLIM WORLD

TOM AND JOANN DOYLE

WITH GREG WEBSTER

W PUBLISHING GROUP

AN IMPRINT OF THOMAS NELSON

Published in Nashville, Tennessee, by W Publishing Group, an imprint of Thomas Nelson.

Thomas Nelson titles may be purchased in bulk for educational, business, fundraising, or sales promotional use. For information, please e-mail SpecialMarkets@ThomasNelson.com.

Unless otherwise noted, Scripture quotations are taken from the Holy Bible, New International Version®, NIV®. © 1973, 1978, 1984, 2011 by Biblica, Inc.® Used by permission of Zondervan. All rights reserved worldwide.

Scripture quotations marked esv are from The Holy Bible, English Standard Version® (ESV®). © 2001 by Crossway, a publishing ministry of Good News Publishers. Used by permission. All rights reserved.

Scripture quotations marked kjv are from the King James Version. Public domain.

The names and identifying details of some of the individuals discussed in this book have been changed to protect their privacy.

Any internet addresses, phone numbers, or company or product information printed in this book are offered as a resource and are not intended in any way to be or to imply an endorsement by Thomas Nelson, nor does Thomas Nelson vouch for the existence, content, or services of these sites, phone numbers, companies, or products beyond the life of this book.

ISBN 978-0-7852-3348-0 (eBook)

Library of Congress Cataloging-in-Publication Data

Names: Doyle, Tom, 1955–, author. | Doyle, JoAnn, author. | Webster, Greg, author.
Title: Women who risk : secret agents for Jesus in the Muslim world / Tom and JoAnn Doyle ; with Greg Webster.
Description: Nashville, Tennessee : W Publishing Group, an imprint of Thomas Nelson, [2021] | Includes bibliographical references. | Summary: "For the first time ever Tom Doyle, popular author and pastor to the unreached, is joined by his wife and ministry partner, JoAnn, to explore the incredible work of God in the hearts and lives of women in the Muslim world. Despite enormous risks to themselves and their families, former Muslim women are now influencing their husbands and their children and bringing others to faith in Jesus Christ. No matter where they live, these women are the God-ordained spiritual gatekeepers of their families"—Provided by publisher.
Identifiers: LCCN 2020032191 | ISBN 9780785233466 (tp) | ISBN 9780785233480 (ebook)
Subjects: LCSH: Women missionaries—Middle East. | Christian converts from Islam. | Missions to Muslims.
Classification: LCC BV2625 .D68 2021 | DDC 266.088/297—dc23
LC record available at https://lccn.loc.gov/2020032191

Printed in the United States of America

23 24 25 26 27 LBC 18 17 16 15 14

*We lovingly dedicate this book to all those who
have lived life in the shadows, who have felt
forgotten, overlooked, unseen, or unheard.
The One who made you sees you and loves you intimately.
His name is Jesus.
You are not forgotten.*

*To those who have found salvation in Jesus
alone and are living a life of risk.
You have counted the cost and risked it all; we
applaud you, for He alone is worthy.*

My mouth will tell of your righteous acts,
of your deeds of salvation all the day,
for their number is past my knowledge.
*With the mighty deeds of the Lord G*OD *I will come;*
I will remind them of your righteousness, yours alone.

—PSALM 71:15–16 ESV

CONTENTS

AN UNSTOPPABLE
FORCE

The most obvious threat to people in the Middle East is terrorism. But recently, that threat has been replaced. And the new one is more intimidating, more terrifying to people there than terrorism.

It's called *change*.

Change can bring adversaries, like Saudi Arabia and Israel, together because of a common enemy, such as Iran. But change can also threaten a religion by targeting its very core.

Although the Convention on the Elimination of All Forms of Discrimination Against Women (CEDAW) was adopted by the United Nations way back in 1979, implementing it in the Middle East has been another matter. Forty years later—in December 2019—some clans in the West Bank claimed that they found CEDAW to be incompatible with the religion of Islam.[1] It would bring too much change.

So we're left to wonder: Will women in the Muslim-dominated Middle East ever be given full rights?

Jesus has answered that question with an emphatic *yes*. And that may be the reason Muslim women are flocking to Him like never before. We believe God has called us to share His miraculous, mind-blowing true stories from the front lines of the Jesus movement in the Middle East with believers around the world.

The responses to my last three books continue to overwhelm JoAnn and me. But it wasn't until we had worked in every country in the Middle East that we realized how badly we needed to write this one.

JoAnn has always been with me in this ministry, and we're always humbled when we meet people who say, "Your stories changed my life." The people we write about are real, and if reading about them changed your life, it's probably because *writing* about them changed ours. But this is the first time JoAnn and I have officially written together. Although she's always been by my side, this time you'll actually hear her voice and gain special insights from her perspective.

I've seen how God prepared JoAnn to bring the light of Jesus to Muslim women throughout the Middle East. She was not initially drawn to them. Sure, she was compassionate toward them, but fear won out and kept her from engaging them wholeheartedly. So believe me when I say that JoAnn can relate to any fears you might have about reaching out to Muslims.

Yet what God calls us to, He prepares us for.

God has brought JoAnn to an astounding level of fearlessness in the most dangerous situations in the Muslim world. The change in her has been thrilling to see. Her Italian, outgoing, loving, and disarming nature has made her a hit wherever we go.

Anne Graham Lotz once told me, "JoAnn may be small in stature, but she's a stick of dynamite for Jesus!"

I agree.

A WORD FROM JOANN

Tom has always had a huge heart for the people who don't know Jesus. Combined with his Indiana Jones spirit and easygoing, winsome ways, he's been a spiritual trailblazer, going where no one else dares to go.

Following 9/11, Tom's first mission to the Gaza Strip opened his eyes anew to the desperate needs and lostness of Muslims. The people he encountered were officially added to the list of those he felt called to reach. Standing by his side in touching these dear souls with the love of Christ has been transformational. Tom has carried on his Irish dad's storytelling ability in his writing, and this book is no different—except if you see a more feminine thought or sugary word, it's probably from me.

BACK TO THE BOOKS

In 2012, I (Tom) wrote *Dreams and Visions: Is Jesus Awakening the Muslim World?* In it we traveled with you around the Middle East to introduce you to former Muslims who experienced high-definition, unshakable dreams and visions of Jesus. Once they had these dreams, each of them went on a quest to understand

Jesus' message. They covertly started reading the Bible or reached out to Christians to learn the message of Jesus' death and resurrection. The eventual salvation experiences of the twenty-five people we wrote about shook up readers in the West who had no idea Muslims were coming to faith in Christ.

In the next book, *Killing Christians: Living the Faith Where It's Not Safe to Believe*, we were passionate for you to meet new believers who were ready to die for Jesus. Many of them did lose their lives and are now being fitted for martyrs' crowns. We also introduced you to the two questions we ask Muslims in the Middle East to determine if they are ready to accept Jesus:

- Are you willing to suffer?
- Are you willing to die for Jesus?

Since Jesus promised we would suffer for Him, we think these are questions that Christians should ask themselves routinely, no matter where they live. We're meeting people from the United States to South America to Europe to the Middle East to Asia who ask themselves those two questions every day.

Next up was *Standing in the Fire: Courageous Christians Living in Frightening Times*, in which we introduced you to saints who thought they were also being fitted for martyrs' crowns. But, miraculously, not one of them died—and not one of them, as of this writing, has been killed. These men and women are in a modern-day fiery furnace, surrounded by Muslim terrorists, but God has made them invincible. Until He calls them to heaven, they will continue flourishing in Christ—not holding back one bit from telling others who Jesus is and leading them to faith, no matter the danger.

And that brings us to this book. *Women Who Risk* will introduce you to some new friends. You'll meet former Muslim women who live in danger but have risen above it, confident in Christ and filled with hope for the future. Since they come from observant Muslim families, they had to decide if they were willing to die for Jesus before they ever accepted Him. To help protect them, we've changed their names and some identifying details, but each story is very real.

For these women, death is the ultimate risk. Yet even in living they face a mother's worst nightmare: Will they lose their children in the process? Nevertheless, the women you'll meet have taken up their crosses (Matt. 16:24) and are model followers of Christ. Each is a modern-day Esther, placed right where she is for this crucial time in history. They share one mission in life: to lead others to Christ, starting with their own families.

All of our women heroes of the faith live in Muslim-majority countries that limit their rights simply because they are female. Their strict Muslim families—many of them fundamentalist—diminish their rights even more.

But God has given women a gift that no family, government, or religion can take from them. They are the *spiritual gatekeepers* of their families. Regardless of their religion—or whether they have one at all—women's spiritual influence is a natural overflow of who God created them to be. As a result of this, God has given women a special kingdom authority.

A man may be called to *lead* the family, but a mother's influence is what *marks* a family. A committed Muslim family almost always has a strong Muslim mother. Considering the lack of rights within the religion for Muslim women, you'd think the opposite would be true. But it's not.

A former imam once told us, "Passing on the Islamic faith to our children was not my job. I read the Qur'an, I prayed five times a day, and I went to Friday prayers at the mosque. All the other stuff was left up to my wife. She was the one who taught the children and trained them to be good Muslims. That was her responsibility, not mine."

AT CREATION

Though Jesus has come to set women free and restore them to their biblical place of honor, the Devil is trying to do just the opposite. He seeks to enslave, oppress, and control them. Ever since the garden of Eden, Satan has held a grudge against women. It was Satan's encounter with Eve that resulted in his judgment, and it was through another woman, Mary, that God sealed Satan's fate in eternity because of the conquering Messiah she bore.

It took just three chapters in the Bible before the Devil launched his all-out assault on women. The destroyer is still trying to settle an old score, and one of his most effective weapons against women today is the religion of Islam, especially the practice and enforcement of Sharia law. Sex trafficking, forced marriages and child brides, molestation, rape, incest, and female genital mutilation are just a few of the horrific abuses women endure within Muslim communities.

The most overlooked, marginalized, and abused person within the religion of Islam lives behind the veil. The history of Islam is seething with mistreatment, cruelty, and a lack of rights for women.

Certainly we're not saying that all Muslims treat women badly or that every Muslim woman experiences this kind of life. But where Sharia law is practiced, Muslim women are second-class citizens, and even non-Muslim women are fair game for forced conversion followed by forced marriage.

And Muslim women who give their lives to Jesus and leave Islam altogether? A quick death sentence is always possible. So who would ever accept Christ and then tell anyone about Him? Yet today that's exactly what an astounding number of women from Muslim communities are doing.

HEAVEN'S CHARGE

Jesus, of course, has a plan. His concern is for souls.

The book of Revelation tells us that all the nations of the world will one day attempt the ultimate rebellion and mount an assault on God. But, until then, Jesus is on a divine rescue mission. Because, to Jesus, *every soul matters.*

During His earthly life, Jesus went out of His way to reach the marginalized, ignored, and despised. He raised eyebrows wherever He went because He ignored the religious elite and honored the "nobodies"—from the demonized man in the Gadarenes to the woman at the well to the ten lepers to tax collectors.

The Messiah not only flipped over the money-changer tables in the temple; He tossed the entire social order out the window, and after our years of working in the Muslim world, we see Jesus doing the same thing with the religion of Islam today. Jesus hasn't forgotten Muslim women, and because of His divine intervention, these new believers are transforming the Middle East.

When Muslim women find Jesus and give their lives to Him, they not only enjoy new freedom in Christ but also become an unstoppable force in the Muslim world. Because women are the spiritual gatekeepers of Islam, and because so many are abandoning their posts to follow Jesus, the front door has been left wide open for entire families to embrace Christ and leave their Muslim faith for good.

Islam is in crisis. Whole families are jumping ship and now following Jesus. Despite the danger, the women endure, and their slow, simmering influence spreads to their children, extended families, and often even their husbands.

Want to see some of this remarkable action for yourself?

Travel with us in the following pages to the Middle East. You'll be thrilled and inspired. These stories will elevate your faith to a new level as you meet your sisters in Christ who live on the front lines of the spiritual war raging in the Middle East.

Like the women at the empty tomb of Christ, Muslim women are discovering that Jesus is alive, and they aren't keeping silent. Some are underground, their influence slow and steady, while others have gone public and yet are surviving the onslaught of persecution from their families and friends for defecting from Islam.

The story of the modern Middle East has taken a new turn. Jesus is setting women free, honoring and elevating them—and they are thriving! And why wouldn't they be? Jesus has arrived. His supporting cast of former Muslim women is raising eyebrows and changing hearts all across the region.

CHAPTER 1

DELIVER US FROM EVIL

Living in Mafraq, Jordan, a mere ten miles from the Syrian border, Omar and Nasreen Kahn were used to hearing explosions at night. But the violence that echoed through their neighborhood this evening came from their own apartment.

Guttural screams and shrieks that made their flesh crawl exploded from the mouth of their twenty-seven-year-old daughter, Nori. The *jinns* were back,[1] and Nori had begun raging just after sundown.

"I hate you and wish you were both dead!" Nori snarled, her face contorted, eyes wide but vacant. "You're miserable human beings and horrible parents!"

Omar and Nasreen cowered in each other's arms, defenseless in the face of a power they knew was beyond them—and their daughter. As they had done countless times before while the Nori Horror Show raged on, they cried out to Allah for help.

Yet Nori only hurled dishes at them in answer to their prayers. A male voice erupting from her throat screamed obscenities that blended with the clamor of shattering dinnerware. Neighbors living within earshot closed their windows against the pandemonium and distracted their children from the deranged sounds coming again from the Kahn household.

SURPRISING ADVICE

"Nurse Kahn to room 217. Stat!"

Nori raced down the second floor of the King Talal Military Hospital, but she was too late. Her favorite patient had expired by the time she reached his room. Working in the cancer unit was stressful and heartbreaking, and Nori couldn't help but think she was responsible whenever one of her patients died.

It's because of the jinns! It has to be. My life is cursed, and everyone I get close to dies. One of these days the hospital staff will figure out how dangerous I am.

Her thoughts clearer following the previous night's evil outburst against her parents, Nori sat in the break room an hour after the death of her patient and stared at her lunch. She shoved olives around her plate with a pita-bread triangle, then jammed the bread into her untouched hummus.

What's wrong with you? the familiar voice hissed in her thoughts. Then she startled at the sound of another voice.

"Nori, are you depressed?" Dr. Jalal Aziz spoke kindly as he sat down in a chair next to her. "I've been in the lunchroom for several minutes, and the expression on your face hasn't changed. I don't want to hurt your feelings, but you look like a stone. I know you've seen several people die in the last few months, but this is the cancer ward, Nori. Unfortunately, that is how it goes around here."

Nori looked around to confirm that the two of them were alone in the break room. Then she took a deep breath, rolled her eyes toward the ceiling, and spoke slowly.

"But why is it that so many of *my* patients are dying? You can't tell me you haven't noticed, Doctor. Something is wrong with me. I'm a bad omen. I feel like the Devil is inside of me."

Nori shifted her gaze from the ceiling and looked into Dr. Aziz's eyes. "There. I said it. I'll probably get fired because you're going to think I've lost my mind, but there's more. Dr. Aziz, I hear voices. I do, and I'm scared because I can't do anything about it."

The physician studied Nori's fearful eyes for several seconds before responding. "Let me tell you something: You're my favorite nurse on this floor. You light up this place. But sometimes, Nori, you sink into a dark hole that seems to take over your whole being."

He shook his head almost imperceptibly. "How can I help you? I really want to know, Nori. Most nurses can only do this job for a few years. It's too much for them."

Placing a finger over his lips, Dr. Aziz leaned toward Nori and whispered, "I want to tell you something else, Nori. You need to go to a church to get help."

The nurse startled in her seat as if she had been slapped. She looked at Dr. Aziz incredulously.

"A church? Dr. Aziz, we are Muslims! Why in the world would either you or I ever go to a church? Christianity is a false religion. It's worthless. Maybe you're the one who has lost your . . . mind." Her own words shocked her.

In return for the insult, Dr. Aziz offered a bare smile. "I knew you were going to say that, Nori. I would've said the same thing a few years ago. Yes, I'm a practicing Muslim, but I don't know one imam who has ever helped anyone hearing voices and being attacked by jinns. Can you name anyone? The 'little people' take over, and the victims they latch onto are never the same."

Nori squeezed her eyes shut; then opening them, she glared at the doctor and blurted words she had never told anyone.

"I was just a little girl when the jinns first came in the night. My father had been in my bedroom, and something evil happened. I just can't remember what it was. I think I was four. I remember seeing my father's face. He had a sinister smile, as if he was making fun of me. Then he left my room, and within minutes I had my first encounter with the jinns. I was terrified of going to sleep from then on. I still am."

Dr. Aziz nodded. "I should not be talking like this, Nori, because your father is a sheikh. He teaches Islam and trains imams. But has *he* helped you? It sounds more to me like your father is part of the problem. He was the one who brought the jinns into your life."

The gravity of Dr. Aziz's point left Nori with nothing to say. She didn't take it personally, nor did she feel shame. It was simply an accurate summary of her situation. Yet the knowledge, for the first time in her life, gave her hope.

FINDING FAITH WITH THE INFIDELS

Nasreen savored the aroma of dark Arabic coffee and eyed her daughter over her second cup.

"Where are you going so bright and early this morning?"

Nori turned at the front door and looked at her mother. "I have a few errands to run before I go to work."

She stepped quickly out the door and sighed. These weren't exactly errands; she had just lied to—or at least seriously misled—her mother.

A twenty-minute walk took her to the entrance of . . . a Roman Catholic church. How had she gotten *this* desperate? How could a Christian church possibly have an answer for her?

"Allah, please end this now!" she prayed aloud; then she bowed her head and stared for several seconds at the sidewalk. She looked up at the church door.

"I know Christians are infidels, and my father would probably kill me for asking a Catholic priest for spiritual advice." Her voice trailed to a whisper. "Save me from the jinns. They are destroying my life."

Nori reached for the badly worn rope dangling from a bell, took a deep breath, and rang the bell hard. She looked again at the ground, fearing she had just made the worst mistake of her life.

The sound of shuffling feet drew her attention to a middle-aged man dressed in black as he limped toward the front gate where she stood. The priest stopped an arm's length from her on the other side of the entryway's eight-foot-high iron bars.

Nori mumbled awkwardly, "I have a problem, and I need help. I hear voices, and they are controlling me at night."

She watched the priest's eyes and was sure she saw a glimmer of compassion. But the man's eyes shifted from side to side. It was his turn for awkwardness, and he spoke slowly, barely above a whisper.

"If I let you in this building, all hell could break loose from the fanatics. I'm sure you understand. You're in danger as well, just by speaking with me here. Someone is probably watching us even now." He breathed deeply. "I'm sure you're a nice person, but this is not the best neighborhood. I'm sorry. I have to go now."

Without waiting for a reply, the sad clergyman turned and walked back into his church.

Nori stared after him. Her hands gripped the iron bars, and she leaned on them as if their support could do for her what the priest would not.

After several minutes, she muttered simply, "I knew they wouldn't help me."

Anger boosted her determination, and Nori headed down Abdul Malik Street into the heart of the Christian section of the city. There were still two hours before she was due at work.

As she reached the corner with Thani Street, a flash of light caught her eye. Midway up the next block, she saw Mafraq's Greek Orthodox church, its gold cross glistening in the sun.

Five minutes later Nori had once again been turned away from the front gate of a church. Another priest, afraid of the potential repercussions of speaking with a Muslim woman, had excused himself because of a "busy day ahead." He, too, had shuffled dejectedly into the church, closed the door behind him, and left Nori wondering what to do next.

Nori was livid and growled quietly to herself, "How dare those Christians do this to me! I thought Jesus was supposed to be so strong. At least that's what the stupid preacher from Egypt said on television last week."

Eight days earlier Nori had been flipping channels. When she came to SAT-7, a voice stopped her.

"Jesus can break every chain."

The words got her attention. She watched a man preach for less than a minute, but it had been long enough to encourage her hope that some Christian somewhere might be able to help her. Now, though, she was fairly certain no Christian could—or at least *would*.

I guess Christians don't really believe Jesus has the power to break chains. Maybe they have their own chains—of fear, I suppose.

"Good morning!"

The greeting interrupted Nori's conversation with herself. She had been staring at the ground but looked up to see a well-dressed couple standing on the sidewalk several feet away. The woman had spoken, and Nori saw her wink at the man before addressing Nori again.

"Are you okay? We saw you walking in circles, and you were talking to . . . well, I guess to yourself. You appear to be a Muslim, and we're wondering if you've gotten lost in the Christian area."

Nori saw such kindness in their eyes that she instantly decided to see if this Christian and her husband—she assumed— could help.

"I have a big problem. I think I need to talk to a Christian pastor or priest or whatever you call them. I've been to two churches already this morning pleading for help to stop the voices I hear that are controlling me. At each church, a man with a priest's collar greeted me, but neither one would help me. They were afraid because—you're right—I'm a Muslim. They were afraid the fundamentalists would see us talking, and the priests would pay the price." Nori shook her head. "You wouldn't know where I could find a pastor, would you?"

The woman smiled warmly and startled Nori with an equally warm hug.

"Do I know a pastor? I'm married to one! This is my husband, Pastor Daniel Hashwa, and I'm Sarah. What's your name?"

"I'm Nori." She laughed and rolled her eyes. "I'm sorry for looking like a crazy person rambling in the street talking to no one. I was ready to give up and never talk to another Christian ever again. I was so angry at those two men."

Daniel leaned toward the woman in the black hijab and asked quietly, "Nori, do you have problems with demons?"

The question was so matter of fact that Nori felt neither offended nor shamed.

"Yes, I do." She nodded calmly, welcoming the opportunity to talk honestly about her problem. "The jinns control me. Who can help?"

Daniel Hashwa smiled, raised his index finger, and beckoned over his shoulder. "Follow me."

Daniel and Sarah led Nori to the Baptist church of Mafraq and into an empty room. Without further conversation, they began praying for the power of Christ to fill the space and set Nori free.

The passion of their prayers astounded Nori as the couple fell to their knees and prayed over their open Bibles. Faces to the ground, they quoted Scripture while Nori sat, wide-eyed, and watched her new friends for a full thirty minutes. Then, abruptly, Daniel and Sarah reached toward Nori and each placed a hand gently on the Muslim woman's shoulder. Nori felt loved as they looked her in the face.

"Nori," Sarah said, "Are you ready to be free?"

"Yes!" Nori shouted as she stood up. "I'll do whatever I have to."

She began to pace. "I'm ready! I've never heard praying like that. How do you do that? Can you teach me?"

Daniel stood up beside her. "Nori, it all starts with Jesus."

Three and a half hours later, the demons were gone. Nori had been released from their torture and her prison. Jinns that had attacked her since she was a child were no match for the overwhelming authority and power of Christ. When Nori left the meeting with Daniel and Sarah, she was a new follower of Jesus.

Before the prayer encounter, Nori had called work and asked for a personal day off. Now she wondered whether she should go in for half a day or go home. After several minutes of debate, she decided to head straight for her parents and face the music. Nori Kahn intended to tell her father and mother that Jesus had set her free.

SITUATION: DESPERATE

As Nori rounded the corner toward her apartment, her jaw dropped. She stopped and stared at red lights flashing halfway down the block. After several seconds, she broke into a run toward the emergency vehicles parked in front of her building. Nori's aunt stood on the sidewalk, chattering into her cell phone.

"Aunt Samira, what's going on?"

The woman stopped talking and shot a glance at her niece. "Nori! We've been looking for you. Where have you been?" She squeezed her eyes shut, quickly rubbed her forehead with her free hand, and then looked straight at Nori. "I'm sorry to tell you this." Her voice softened. "Your father is dead."

Nori gasped and sprinted into the apartment. She found her mother sitting on the living-room floor and threw herself into Nasreen's arms.

"Your father came home early from *Jummah* at the mosque."[2] Nori's mother choked out the words. "He said he didn't feel good, so I told him to lie down. Two hours later, I went into our room to check on him, and he wouldn't . . . he wouldn't move. Nori, if I'd known he was that sick, I would've done something. I was in the kitchen doing dishes while your father was in the bedroom *dying*."

Nasreen bawled. "It's all my fault! I could've saved his life, and I did nothing. My precious Omar—why did you have to leave me?"

Nori gripped her mother in a desperate hug but said nothing. Her thoughts raced. How could the day she met Jesus—the best day of her life—have taken such a disastrous turn? Yes, Omar Kahn had brought terrible things into her life, but nevertheless, he was her father. And now he was gone.

LIFE AFTER THE DEATH

Family and friends arrived from all over Jordan to pay respects to the Kahn family. They set aside petty arguments over King Abdullah's politics and Islamic theology, and no one spoke harshly about anything. Nori relished the time of family peace. She longed, though, to tell about her exciting new faith in Jesus, to share her redeemed life with a few family members she thought might be receptive.

Her twentysomething cousins, she knew, were thoroughly fed up with Islam, and she was ready to burst with the good news. But, strangely, Nori felt the Spirit of God impress her not to talk openly right now. The time for that would somehow come later.

During her father's traditional burial service, people read passages from the Qur'an. They closed Omar's eyes and mouth, bathed his body, and shrouded him in a plain white cloth. Muslim clerics prayed that Omar's sins would be forgiven. Visiting clergy honored the influential sheikh and sat with the family. Finally, wrapped only in the burial cloth, Omar's body was placed directly in the ground and turned to face south, toward Mecca.

Nori struggled to make sense of the week's events. The jinns were gone, but the very same day Daniel and Sarah had commanded them to leave, her father died. There had to be a connection.

Even though Nori had known Jesus for just a few days, she knew she had found a better way. Nori saw it in the funeral service that lacked all hope and wondered how she had missed this obvious void at other burials she'd been to. It was depressing. Her father had spent his entire life worshiping Allah alone and honoring the prophet Muhammad, yet there was no assurance that he had done enough to enter paradise.

There were no answers, only questions. Every eye was downcast, faces overtaken by worry and grief. She sensed that everyone felt as if, somehow, Omar, only forty-nine years old, had provoked the wrath of Allah and been taken out.

Nori wanted to stand up and scream, "It doesn't have to be this way! Islam is not the way. Jesus is!"

But she kept silent.

After a week of collective mourning, the last visiting family members left the Kahn apartment. Even though Nori's father had treated her badly most of her life, she was surprised at how much she missed his presence.

Her new knowledge of Jesus had opened her eyes to new knowledge about her earthly father as well. During her prayer time with Daniel and Sarah, the Holy Spirit had prompted her memory: Omar Kahn had begun abusing Nori when she was only four years old.

The memories confirmed Dr. Aziz's suspicion that the jinns were connected to her father. But now she was free—and her father was gone. The pain of her past could no longer enslave her. The voices that accused her were silent.

Nori had fire in her heart to tell others. But how could she while living in the strict Muslim community of Mafraq? If she wasn't careful, her new life would be very short.

She also wondered where to begin. Questions rambled through her mind:

- *How can I share Jesus with people who, like me, were raised in Islam?*
- *How many Muslim girls have been molested?*
- *Don't these girls have questions like I did?*
- *Are other children captive to the demons?*
- *How can I bring young Muslims the good news without getting killed—possibly even by someone in my own family?*

Alone in her bedroom one night the week after her father's death, she prayed aloud but quietly, "Lord, let me tell my generation! How can I be a light for You, Jesus?"

Just then a friend request pinged on Nori's Facebook account, and she had her answer.

NORI, THE NEW FORCE

One month later Nori had devoured the Bible given to her at the discipleship group she attended daily at lunchtime. Since the King Talal Military Hospital wasn't far from the Baptist church, Nori could race there by taxi and easily be back in time for her afternoon shift. Fundamentalists were always on the lookout for apostates, so she checked for Muslim men with long beards every time she entered the church. Whenever she spotted someone suspicious, she evaded him, but nothing would stop her. She never missed a lesson.

Nori not only studied Scripture; she memorized as many of the wondrous new words as she could manage. Each night, she stayed up until the early morning hours reading and praying. She lay on her face and cried out to God for her mother, her family, and her friends. Matthew 7:7–8 became especially powerful for her: "Ask and it will be given to you; seek and you will find; knock and the door will be opened to you. For everyone who asks receives; the one who seeks finds; and to the one who knocks, the door will be opened."

After a month of study and prayer, she was ready. She'd been planning this from the moment the timely Facebook request had answered her question about sharing her life with others.

Nori sat in front of the computer at her bedroom desk and prayed, "Lord Jesus, once again, I ask You to give me my generation. Young Muslims are dead inside. They are lost, lonely, and hurting—just like I was. I must go to them. I know where they are, and I know how to find them. I want to see them set free and their chains broken.

"I'm ready to go. Whatever happens—good or bad—I give this to You. Here I am, Lord. Send me!"

Nori selected from her cell-phone files a photo in which her face, except for her eyes, was fully covered by the black niqab she'd worn when going to the mosque for Friday prayers. She logged on to a new Facebook account she had created earlier that evening and launched "Huda Has Hope." Her first post read:

Good evening, everyone! My name is Huda. Why do I have hope? Because I *found the Truth*.

Come discover the real Truth with me. I'll be here every night and will do my best to answer your questions. I just recently found the Truth, so I'm not an expert. But I am passionate about my new faith. I have a story to tell. Will you join me? Our journey begins tomorrow night. Tell your friends. Everyone is welcome. This is a shame-free zone. All questions are welcome. Except one. I'm not looking for a husband! So no marriage proposals, okay? See you tomorrow night!

Nori logged off and took a deep breath.

The next day at King Talal Military Hospital, Dr. Aziz approached his favorite nurse.

"Nori, when we talked a month ago, you had the heaviest

heart I'd ever seen. I was worried about you, but something's happened. You're the happiest nurse on the second floor—maybe in the whole hospital! You're a different person. What's new?"

"Dr. Aziz," Nori said with a grin, "I just followed doctor's orders. I did what you told me to do."

Dr. Aziz gaped. "You went to a church?"

"I did. But more importantly, I gave my life to Jesus. I'm not a Muslim anymore, and I'm free from demons, Dr. Aziz. Jesus defeated the works of the Devil; they have no grip on me anymore."

Dr. Aziz grabbed Nori's arm, pulled her into a side hallway, and spoke in a loud whisper.

"I'm thankful you're free from what was dragging you down, Nori, but you've got to be careful. When you said, 'I gave my life to Jesus. I'm not a Muslim anymore,' it was loud enough to be heard all the way down the hall. There are many committed Muslims in this hospital—and Jordanian soldiers too. Please don't broadcast this. You could get yourself hurt or killed." The doctor shook his head and smirked. "I think I'm more worried about you now than when you were fighting demons."

"I'll be fine, Dr. Aziz. And thank you for your concern. I will be careful, too, but I can't help myself. I want all Muslims to know Jesus like I do. Can we talk on a break tomorrow? You've got to hear my story. The last time we visited, you helped me. Maybe this time I can help you."

Nori tapped her chest twice, then skipped down the hall.

That night at dinner, Nasreen noticed her daughter's joy.

"Nori, did you have a really good day at work or something? You're ready to jump out of your shoes."

"Mom, I have so much to tell you—and I will—but I've got an appointment I can't be late for. Can we talk tomorrow at dinner? Just you and me, maybe?"

Nasreen agreed, and Nori excused herself from the table. She went to her room and quietly locked the door behind her. As Huda Has Hope logged on to Facebook, she noticed that 103 people had already friended her.

Nori offered a quick prayer. "Oh, Lord, give me the words, just like You gave Daniel and Sarah when I needed them. There are more than a hundred people waiting for answers that You have for them. Please communicate through me."

She began typing.

Good evening. This is Huda Has Hope. Two months ago, I was a mess. I had horrific nightmares, and jinns attacked me at night. I wanted to kill myself. Today, I am a new person. So here is my story. If you relate to anything I share tonight, I sure want to hear from you. Maybe, just maybe, you have the same questions I did.

I always felt an emptiness in my heart. Something was missing—or Someone was missing. Tonight, I tell you my journey . . . to Jesus.

Nori published the post. Now it was out there. She closed her eyes and prayed for her new friends online.

Her opening words triggered a torrent of comments:

"Infidel!"

"I hate you!"

"You deserve to die!"

But once the initial salvos abated, more receptive responses chimed in:

"Keep going, Huda! Tell us your story."

"Don't let them intimidate you. Keep going."

"I am so frustrated with religion. Especially our religion."

"Women can have a voice too!"

"Tell me about Jesus. I live in Saudi Arabia."

Nori posted again.

Marhaba![3] I'm glad to see so many of you with me tonight. It looks like it will be a lively conversation. I'll try to answer questions when I finish my story. I want you to know that I love all of you—even the ones who have sent me threats.

So back to my story. I got tired of religion: do this, do that. Was it ever enough? Well, it wasn't. If even the prophet Muhammad wasn't sure he would make it to heaven, how could I ever have this assurance? The answer is that I could not.

Here's what Muhammad said [Qur'an 46:9]: "I am no bringer of new-fangled doctrine among the messengers, nor do I know what will be done with me or with you."[4]

But then I met Jesus, who said this: "Therefore brothers and sisters, since we have confidence to enter the Most Holy Place by the blood of Jesus . . . let us draw near to God" [Heb. 10:19, 22].

Muhammad didn't know if he would gain heaven. But Jesus said
He was the *Way* to heaven.

For the next three hours, Huda Has Hope answered question
after question the best she could. Nori quoted the Bible and gra-
ciously deflected threats by demonstrating how "a gentle answer
turns away wrath" (Prov. 15:1).

Well after midnight, Nori decided it was time for bed.
Tomorrow would be a big day. Telling Nasreen about her new life
would not be easy. As she drifted off to sleep, Nori prayed that
her mother would be as receptive as some of her new friends on
Facebook.

TESTING THE WATERS

Nasreen Kahn listened quietly to her daughter's story. But when
she could no longer ignore the rage boiling inside of her, she stood,
reached a balled hand across the dinner table, and punched Nori
full in the face. The younger woman sprawled backward, knees
upending the table as she fell. Kabobs and baba ghanoush splat-
tered the wall behind Nori. Shocked by her mother's sudden
reaction, she simply stared up at her from the floor as Nasreen
launched into a tirade.

"You're a disgrace to this family! Your father would be more
ashamed of you than I can say—a man of such importance in the
Jordanian community. We are *Muslims*, Nori. You will *never* be a
Christian, or a follower of Jesus, or whatever you call it!" She spat the
words. "You are weak. But you will come to your senses and realize
you were born a Muslim, and you will die a Muslim. Is that clear?"

To Nasreen, it was a rhetorical question, and she continued without pausing for an answer. "Do I need to call your cousins to come and beat some sense into you? I will phone them right now, Nori, and they will be glad to finish what I started."

"Momma, I think you've made your point quite clearly."

Nori pulled herself from off the floor, then walked past her mother. At the kitchen door she turned and smiled politely. Then she stumbled to her room, closed the door, and locked it. Huda had new friends waiting for her, but before she attended to them, Nori dropped to her knees, forgave her mom, and opened the Bible.

Huda's friends list had grown to more than two hundred, and for the rest of the evening, Huda Has Hope shared her heart and Jesus' love. At one o'clock in the morning, she switched off her computer.

A NEW ROUTINE

For the next month, little changed in the Kahn apartment. Each time Nori arrived home, Nasreen screamed curses at her only daughter. There was no dinner; her mother reminded Nori every night that she didn't deserve it.

"You can starve for all I care!"

The only reprieve Nori had was in her bedroom behind a locked door. As soon as Nori shut out her mother's hate speech, Huda was online spreading the love of Jesus.

After three months Huda Has Hope had more than one thousand friends, but Nori's mother had not wavered. Nori couldn't believe her mom could come up with fresh curses to blister her, but each time, she would wait until her mom was finished and then say sweetly, "I still love you very much, Mom."

The online needs were so pressing and numerous that Nori managed only about four hours of sleep a night. Hundreds waited for her every evening, and the array of friends dotted every corner of the Middle Eastern map—Cairo, Baghdad, Damascus, Jerusalem, Gaza City, Tehran. There were even several from Mecca and Medina.

Nori loved her lunchtime Bible lessons at church, but the rest of each day at the hospital was grueling. More people than ever seemed to be in the last stages of cancer.

The resulting toll of hospital tragedies and lack of sleep left Nori so drained that she didn't think she could manage another night staying up late to answer questions. But every time she opened her Facebook page, the enormous needs of her broken and hurting friends gripped her heart.

At three o'clock in the morning on one particularly taxing night of answering questions, Nori could barely keep her eyes open. She was about to shut down her page when a new friend request flashed onto the screen. Nori stared at her computer. Could it be?

The name on the request was *Nasreen*.

Nori Shares Her Shocking Surprise

My mother had no idea she was asking questions of her own daughter.

When I first saw my mother's name pop up, I didn't connect that it could actually *be* my mother. She was so hostile toward me day after day.

Then the new friend wrote, **My name is Nasreen Kahn.
I have many questions. Can you help me?**

I literally fell out of my chair and sat on the floor for
several minutes before I could compose myself. I thanked
God that He had touched my mom's heart. I remember
saying out loud, "Jesus, You are the One who hears all
prayers!"

I had prayed for my mom, but she was so hard, so full
of hatred toward me. She seemed like a lost cause.

Yet her questions were not angry ones. My mother
truly wanted to know about Jesus.

Can you believe that? I was in my room; my mom was
in her room, and she never imagined that she was chatting
with me just a few feet away.

The first night she asked me a sincere question from
her heart: **Huda, does Jesus always change people and
fill their hearts with love?**

I wanted to run out of my room, hug Mom, and tell
her it was me. But the Holy Spirit moved me to stay online,
answer her questions, and not reveal myself to her—yet. I
knew I was to stick to the gospel and lift up Jesus.

I realize now that the whole thing could have gone
sideways if I'd blown my cover. I was Huda to my mom,
and it had to stay that way. In a sense, she was under-
cover too.

The questions continued for about a month. She
asked everything you can imagine. Things such as **Isn't
the Bible corrupted?** and **Why do Christians worship
three gods?** I did my best to answer each question one
by one.

Even though Nasreen had questions for Huda every night, when I would come home, Mom would ignore or yell at me, Nori. Then I'd go to my room and Mom to hers. That's when our conversations became amazing.

And then it happened. I burst into tears when my mom asked me this: **I want so badly to have what my daughter has. She has love in her heart and radiates joy. I want that in my life. But I'm so afraid. I am truly frightened at what will happen to me. What do I do?**

I could hardly stay put. I wanted to run out of the room and shout, "Momma, it's me!" But again, Jesus calmed my heart, and I stayed at my computer. I felt Jesus saying, *Bring her to Me, Nori. You can do this.*

And He was right. Once we were through with her questions that night, I prayed with my mother to give her life to Jesus. My computer was drenched in my tears by the time I finished leading my mother to Christ—on Facebook Messenger!

Was this a dream? I wondered that after we prayed. But it was real. Even though I wanted to go hug my mom, I knew it was still not time to tell her.

From then on, Mom was a different person! The next night when I came home, she met me at the door with the biggest smile I'd ever seen on her face. I walked in and was astounded to see the table filled with food. She had been cooking all day.

Still, I waited. I didn't tell my mother that I was Huda Has Hope for another two weeks. But when I did, the timing—God's timing—was perfect.

REUNITED—FOR THE FIRST TIME

Nori's heart pounded in her chest. She knew the time had come to tell her mother.

Nori avoided any subject of significance during dinner, but as the two women stood in the kitchen washing dishes, Nori turned to Nasreen and blurted, "Momma, I want you to know something: I'm getting baptized this Sunday."

Nasreen stopped washing and looked at her daughter, her eyes sparkling with love.

"Nori, I think that's wonderful. I'm proud of you!"

Nori absorbed the unimaginable words and began to sob. She saw that her mother's hatred was truly gone and that Nasreen, too, was free in Jesus. She was a new woman.

Wresting control of her emotions, Nori looked softly at her mother and confessed, "Momma, I'm Huda. It was me all along."

Nasreen's mouth fell open just enough to register shock. Then her face glowed as if she had unwrapped the best present she'd ever received. Nasreen grabbed her daughter and lifted her off the floor, twirling her as if she were a little girl again.

"Oh, Nori! I'm so sorry for all the anger I had toward you. I yelled at you, cursed you, threw food at you. I'm ashamed of myself." She set her daughter down. "And all you did was love me back. You were like Jesus to me. Just like Him!"

The following Sunday afternoon, as Pastor Daniel had promised during Bible study that week, the church was set up for baptism. Doors were locked to avoid unwanted visitors because the converts were all former Muslims with families who might try to kill the apostates from Islam. But the new followers of Christ came in obedience to believe and be baptized.

Nori's Sweet Ending

That Sunday, my mother was in the first row, clapping and crying when I was baptized. Who could've imagined that?

As we walked out of the church, my mom had her arm around me and asked me a question: "Nori, when is the next baptism? I'm ready."

I was shocked yet again, but Pastor Daniel overheard the conversation. He winked at me, and I knew what he meant.

I turned to Mom and told her, "Momma, the next baptism is right now!"

We made a U-turn and headed back into the church. This time I was in the front row.

Now, my mother and I send our love to you from Jordan. We love Jesus. He is everything to us. What a joy to study the Bible and pray together.

Please remember this: Muslims are searching for a relationship with God that only Jesus can give. Pray for them! Often, the people who fight you the most and are the angriest when you share Christ with them are the ones who are feeling the most convicted. I saw this in my mother. Her animosity and rage toward me were just a cover for the insecurity she had deep in her heart. The Devil tried everything he could to keep me from giving her Jesus' sweet words of life. He lost. Jesus won!

My mother and I both have hope now. We really do. We found the Truth, and it's all because of Jesus.

Behold, at that time I will deal
    with all your oppressors.
And I will save the lame
    and gather the outcast,
and I will change their shame into praise
    and renown in all the earth.
      —ZEPHANIAH 3:19 ESV

CHAPTER 2

THE WORST MARRIAGE IN SYRIA

Dina Hadad wrapped the Islamic head covering thoughtfully around her twenty-nine-year-old face, folded her arms across her chest, and found herself fantasizing again. She wasn't dreaming of another man. She was dreaming of how she could kill the one she was married to and get away with it.

She contemplated the glistening edge of a butcher knife, inert on the kitchen counter. Tempted as she was to accelerate plans for murdering her husband, she recoiled from the thought of the grisly images she'd see—and the violence her children would no doubt witness—if she were to hack Mohammad to death.

Noises in the bedroom mingled with the sound of Arabic love songs playing softly on the television in the now-empty living room. They drew her thoughts from the knife back to what

27

was unfolding around her. Another night of enduring the sounds of her husband in the arms of yet another woman. Her upper lip curled involuntarily. Perhaps she could kill them both and simply forfeit any hope of getting away with the crime.

LIFE IN THE KILL ZONE

Dina had lived all of her twenty-nine years in Aleppo, Syria. She hoped she would die there, and, until recently, she'd hoped it would happen soon.

I hate my life!

How many times had she had that thought? Every few minutes for every one of the past nine years of her marriage? Yes. That would be thousands of times.

Glancing out the front window of her second-story apartment a couple of weeks earlier, Dina had sighed and pulled the head covering more tightly around her delicate face. It was a reflexive act of self-protection in response to the moment she most dreaded each day. Mohammad was home.

Mohammad Hadad marched angrily up the outside stairs and shoved open the front door. He stood for a second on the threshold, eyes narrowing as they adjusted to the interior lighting. Stepping into the living room, he twisted his upper body, exaggerating the movement necessary to slam the door shut. Without a word, he scanned the room until his eyes found Dina.

It was *the look*. Dina sucked in her breath, knowing the terror that would blacken the night. The Hadad children, six-year-old Jabar and seven-year-old Maha, had fled to their rooms as soon as the front door had opened. Dina confronted Mohammad's contorted face alone. Perhaps, she thought, she could disarm the coming attack with an ingratiating request.

"Mohammad."

Dina forced a smile as her husband approached her at the kitchen doorway.

"I would like to run to the souk and get us some fresh, hot bread for dinner. Do I have your permission?"

Force from the man's fist to the right side of her head sent her careening backward into the small kitchen. As she fell, the left side of her face slammed into the metal sink.

Several minutes later, Dina became aware of cold tile from the floor touching her cheek. Blood, still streaming from her nose, had pooled beside her. The misery she endured each day in her marriage was worse than typical life in Aleppo, even though the city was a war zone.

Suicide, she'd previously concluded, was her only hope for relief—but in this moment she'd realized, in a bold glimpse of the obvious, that she was not necessarily the one who had to die for her marriage nightmare to end. Mohammad had beaten her once too often. Dina began to form a new plan in her mind.

Syria's largest metropolis hadn't always been a pile of rocks and bombed-out buildings. In its long history, there had been many magnificent years.

Sitting just over halfway from the majestic cliffs of Burj Islam on the Mediterranean Sea to the broad sweep of the Euphrates River in the region's richest watershed, Aleppo hosted some of the most lucrative trade routes in the ancient world. Thanks to the Silk Road, Aleppo became an affluent trade center, and the people groups who ruled there were a who's who of history. Hittites, Assyrians, Greeks, Romans, and Ottomans each capitalized on the city's steady stream of imports—and the associated income— before being displaced by the next dynasty.[1] Indeed, Aleppo may be one of the oldest and most continuously inhabited cities in the world. Some historians believe it is eight thousand years old.[2]

When the Syrian civil war began, however, Aleppo's wealth was decimated. Its lucrative position along a trade route had morphed into the epicenter of a grueling, horrific battlefront that invited troops from Russia, Iran, America, and Israel, as well as virulent powers, such as ISIS and Jabhat al-Nusra. Rockets, bombs, mortars, and gunfire between terrorist rebel groups, the official Syrian government, and the international contestants daily erased historical sites, mosques, and churches. The United Nations Office for the Coordination of Humanitarian Affairs (OCHA) estimated that it would take "six years of continuous work" just to clear the debris in Aleppo.[3]

Dina did her best to ignore the daily bedlam. The threat of sarin gas, the potential kidnapping of her children, and the scarcity of food and water were external dangers she had learned to endure.

The battle she was losing, however, was the one within the walls of her own home. The stress of it was exterminating her soul. Other than her children, only Dina's younger sister, Aisha, knew the full extent of her sufferings.

"What? Should I be grateful that the beatings are not every day—just *most* days?"

Dina had poured out her heart to Aisha on their way to noon prayers one Friday shortly after her realization.

"He treats me cruelly and then does his best to make sure I bear more children for him. What kind of a monster does that?"

Aisha recognized where the conversation was leading.

"Dina, you can't kill Mohammad and expect to get away with it. Did you forget one little detail? You're a woman! Men do the honor killings in our religion, not the other way around. For us, it's just murder, and you'd be lucky if all they did was behead you."

"Aisha, it's not just for me. I pray every day that Allah will keep Mohammad from turning his evil temper on my precious children. They don't deserve a home like this. No child does. Yet with every abuse, Mohammad justifies himself with surahs from the Qur'an. What does that teach Jabar and Maha about our religion?"

Dina stopped walking and looked at Aisha, then stared past the people streaming toward the mosque.

"Maybe it teaches them the truth." Dina spoke as if in a daze. "What a religion this is! Are women just born to be slaves, punching bags, and baby machines?" She turned back to Aisha. "Is that our lot? Our *calling*?"

A wry smile crept onto Dina's face.

"Aisha, it won't leave a trace, and best of all, Mohammad will linger long enough to feel real pain." She nodded with satisfaction. "I've figured it out. Poisoning someone's food is easy, and it will look like he just had a heart attack. By the time anyone notices Mohammad is missing the next morning, I'll be having breakfast in Beirut with Jabar and Maha."

"Dina, that's nonsense! You will *not* get away with this.

Mohammad may not love you, but I do, and I don't want to lose you. He's not worth what it would cost you." Aisha shook her head emphatically. "You're delusional. Please tell me you'll never actually try this.

"Besides," Aisha added, "Jummah is here. How can we even be thinking of these things on our way to Friday prayers? May Allah not strike us both dead!"

"I wish he would!" Dina shouted at her sister as she stormed into the human flow.

"Shush, you fool!"

Dina's eyes flashed. "Aisha, I've prayed all my life for a good marriage, and this is what I get? Beatings, constant degradation, other women in my bed, and one hundred percent control by my husband? No, Aisha. Allah is too busy to pay attention to me. Either that, or I'm not important enough to matter to him."

Dina turned and walked slowly up the sidewalk. She spoke as if to herself. "Or, just maybe, we pray to the wrong God, Aisha. Have you ever thought of that?"

Aisha pressed the fingers of her right hand to her forehead. "Dina, once we walk into our mosque, this conversation is over. In fact, I want to forget about it permanently. You'll be better off too. As if it never happened."

The two women crossed the threshold of the Great Mosque.

"Good afternoon, Sheikh Husseini." Aisha greeted the seventy-year-old imam and cut her eyes toward Dina, pleading with her to stop the rant. Then she turned toward the mosque's section for women, pulled off her shoes, and slipped them into a vacant cubby alongside dozens of others.

Inside the cavernous assembly room five minutes later, the elderly cleric intoned Friday prayers. Several hundred voices joined him: "Guide us along the straight path—the path of those whom you favored, not of those who earned your anger or went astray." The memorized words rolled off Dina's tongue, but they were the words of a zombie, not from the heart of a woman.

Forty-five minutes later Aisha pulled her shoes from the rack and headed out of the mosque, intent on controlling the conversation with Dina on the walk home.

"Dina, how proud I am of our religion. Even though the thousand-year-old minaret was destroyed by the Free Syrian Army, we will rebuild. I know we will. Sunni Islam is the purest Muslim religion.

"The repulsive Alawite government of our vile president, Bashar al-Assad, will not stop us. He's barely hanging on to power as it is. I see a day when one of ours will be president of Syria. Assad is pathetic, and without Iran propping him up, he'd be dead by now. I hate the Alawites!

"But not as much as I hate those Christians. Because of the war, they're leaving our city like scared donkeys. They can *all* go as far as I'm concerned."

Dina rolled her eyes at the younger woman. "Aisha, every time you come out of Jummah, your anger is alarming." She raised her left eyebrow. "Maybe *you* should've married Mohammad. You might be his match."

Aisha's eyes narrowed. "I'm not the one talking about killing someone, *sister.*"

Dina's expression relaxed for the first time since the two women had met more than an hour earlier. She chuckled.

"You've got a point." Dina aimed her right index finger at Aisha. "But you're beginning to sound like Sheikh Husseini. And he scares me." She shook her head. "No wonder

Mohammad loves him so. But did you notice that he toned down the rhetoric today? I'm guessing he had to, with all of Assad's secret police combing the town. I wonder how many were at the mosque. His spies are some of the most faithful Muslims in Syria. They never miss Friday prayers! And I'm sure they never miss reporting every word the imams and sheikhs say in their sermons."

Aisha merely scowled and said little on their remaining stroll home.

TEMPORARY WIVES, PERMANENT SCARS

"Hi, Momma!"

Two children bounced into the kitchen, drawing Dina back to the present. She picked up the butcher knife and shoved it into a drawer by the sink. Thankfully, the children had grown immune to muted noises from the bedroom when their father had a guest. Just to be sure, though, as she usually did on such evenings, Dina shooed the two siblings out the door for a short walk to Aunt Aisha's apartment.

Maha and Jabar were often mistaken for twins, but Maha was ten months older than her brother. For the Hadad children, it was always a good day when they went straight to Aunt Aisha's apartment after school, which was becoming more frequent.

"Your aunt Aisha has some fresh basbousa that she made just for you and nobody else!⁴ We may even eat dinner with her."

Dina jogged with the children down the street, but her smile hid a heart that was breaking for them. Her sweet, innocent children did not deserve to endure the narcissism their father claimed was his right as a faithful Muslim man.

The three of them ran up the stairs to Aisha's fourth-floor apartment. Their aunt knew why they were there even before Dina said a word. Maha and Jabar raced to claim their servings of basbousa while Aisha pulled Dina into the living room.

"Mohammad is a creep, Dina! I've been thinking it over, and I'm with you, sister. After all he's put you through, I will laugh and dance the day he dies. Is tonight's 'love' a new girlfriend or the same one from last week?"

Dina closed her eyes in shame and disgust before answering.

"The same," she murmured. "I saw her car—no doubt a prize from all the money she makes as a temporary wife. You know as well as I do that she can't possibly be attracted to him." Dina sneered.

"Unless she's blind," Aisha chortled, patting her sister on the shoulder as she headed back to the kitchen. She would need to stretch dinner for three extra people tonight.

From the balcony of Aisha's apartment, sometime after nine o'clock, Dina noticed that the evening visitor's car was gone from the street in front of the Hadad apartment. Mohammad's encounter was over, so she gathered the children for their walk down the vacant street.

Dina wasn't afraid of the bombs—they were too far away to harm them tonight—and she expected there was no reason to fear Mohammad this evening either. He would be in a great mood, ready to bluster about his latest conquest. What a perverse sham of a marriage she had shared with dozens of other women.

As she pushed open the front door of her apartment, a smile rippled across her face in response to her favorite thought these days: *Oh, how I love the image of seeing him dead.*

"Maha and Jabar!" Mohammad's voice boomed from the hallway. "Come give Daddy a hug!"

He presented himself, open armed, at the living-room door.

"Have you had a good day? Daddy sure did! Another business deal came through. You should be proud. All three of our family corporations are making huge profits—even in the midst of the war. I had to celebrate a little after such a stellar day."

He turned to their mother. "And how are you, Dina? Did you enjoy your evening out?"

Dina's stomach churned. At the sound of Mohammad's voice, Aisha's fine meal soured in her belly, and she felt nauseous just looking at her husband. He was about to offer the usual recitation about his relationship of the evening.

"Dina, my *mut'ah* contract has all the signatures.[5] You know I always follow the rules for a temporary marriage." He drew in a deep breath. "What a remarkable religion we have that recognizes men have needs that must be met. Sheikh Husseini gave his full approval, of course." He winked. "Hadiya approved too. She says I'm quite the lover.

"My extra activity has made me feel especially romantic tonight toward my fine wife!"

Mohammad stood facing Dina, a devilish grin on his face. Dina turned, bolted into the kitchen, and threw up in the sink.

THE PLOT TAKES SHAPE

The next morning Dina and Aisha met for a walk up and down their neighborhood streets. After hearing Dina's account of the previous evening, Aisha shook her head.

"I admit it, Dina: I do love everything about Islam, except mut'ah. It may be part of our religion, but it is pure evil." She put her hand to her forehead. "And to think some women make a living doing this! How sick a profession is that?" Aisha paused. "This can't be from our religion. It must have started in the West—probably in America."

Dina glanced sideways at her sister. "Aisha, it *is* from our religion! Believe me, Mohammad has made that clear. The only surahs he knows are the ones about male privilege and sex. He loves to say, 'The Great Prophet had thirteen wives.'"

"Yah, like your husband is a prophet. He's just a sex addict using our religion as a cover. Our Great Prophet was entitled to his thirteen wives, Dina."

"And why is that, Aisha? I used to believe that myself but not anymore. You sound like a good Muslim man with your reasoning about the Prophet. For centuries, Muslim women have had to put up with this perversity all because of him."

"Dina! How dare you!" Aisha raised her right hand as if to slap her sister.

Dina stopped walking, turned toward the younger woman, and stabbed the air with her index finger. "Just so you know, Aisha, my religious, fundamentalist, prophet-honoring husband has had even more wives than the Great One. And he keeps track of them just like he does his business." She paused for effect. "Mohammad has a ledger."

Aisha gasped.

"Yes. Mohammad is so full of himself that he loves to tell about each new woman. As of last night, he has had a grand total of sixty-six wives."

Aisha froze in her tracks. After several seconds she found words, faced her sister, and blurted, "Kill him! I'll help you get rid of Mohammad, my sister. I'll even buy the rat poison."

SAVED BY THE WAR

Mohammad Hadad woke up in a cold sweat. He reached for his sleeping wife.

"Dina, I just had another dream about a Man in a white robe. Who is He?"

Eyes closed, Dina muttered, "I don't know, Mohammad. Go back to sleep, please."

Still brooding over his dream, Mohammad lay still and listened to the sound of distant explosions. After several minutes, he became aware that the noise had stopped. The eerie silence made his flesh crawl. Suddenly the shock wave from a massive explosion in the street outside the apartment rocked the building and blew out the bedroom window. Shards of glass sprayed the walls.

Both Hadad children shrieked. Mohammad heard hysterical children in the adjacent apartments and people crying in the street below. Dina bolted upright as Maha and Jabar lunged into the bed.

In the chaos, Mohammad realized the cell phone was ringing, and his eyes widened. It was the call he'd been waiting for—praying for.

He answered and listened briefly, as if taking orders, then clicked off the phone and grabbed his wife's arm.

"Dina, take Jabar and Maha, and go to your parents' place! You'll be safer on the other side of the city. Tonight is the night! Our Muslim brothers have come together to defeat, once and for all, Bashar al-Assad's forces. Those filthy Alawites and other fallen Muslims were duped into serving that pig of a leader. But we will annihilate them—every last one!" His eyes drilled into Dina. "Take the car *and go!*"

Minutes later Dina threw into the car a suitcase stuffed with several days' worth of clothing for her and the children. She marshaled Jabar and Maha into the back seat, then scrambled behind the steering wheel. While explosions echoed from neighboring streets, Dina gunned the engine and roared off toward her parents' home.

Less than a mile later, Dina and the two children slowed to a crawl. A flood of cars jammed streets heading away from the battlefront, the overflow further impeded by roadblocks.

Dina spotted an opening into the parking lot of a grocery store and raced through the nearly empty space to an alley behind the building. She sped along the narrow route, avoiding several checkpoints, and found an open road west toward her parents' house. She could hardly believe her good fortune.

She had badly needed a break and got one. She was not only away from the fighting but was also free of Mohammad. With any luck he would be killed tonight—or at least in the next few days—along with the rest of his terrorist friends. And even if he survived, Dina would never come back. The corner of her mouth turned up in the barest of smiles. For an instant, she actually felt bad for Mohammad. But *just* for an instant.

MOHAMMAD'S MIRACLE

"Aisha." Dina gripped the steering wheel with one hand while holding the cell phone in her other hand. "Where are you? Please tell me that *your* husband was not foolish enough to stay and fight the Syrian army."

"No, Dina, he didn't. Abdullah is with me, and we're almost to Mom and Dad's. Is Mohammad with you?"

"No, he stayed and is prepared to fight to the death."

Dina puzzled at the long pause, then understood when she read the text from Aisha. Her sister had not wanted Abdullah to hear her response, and Dina nearly dropped the phone, laughing as she read the words **I'll cancel my trip to the store for rat poison.**

Dina clicked off the call and, for the second time that night, felt a tinge of sadness for the man she had been planning to kill.

Miles from the home of Dina's parents, Mohammad and new recruits of the Free Syrian Army (FSA) gathered to receive their orders. Although Mohammad wasn't an official member of the terrorist group, his three businesses helped fund their attacks, and the steady stream of cash he contributed had kept him off the front lines for the past three-and-a-half years.

But those days were over.

An extraordinary collection of President Assad's former generals stood before a packed room. All of them had recently defected, and as a result, Aleppo would soon be subject to the ferocity of their revenge. FSA rebels held the east side of the city while the Syrian government held the west side, battle lines clearly laid out by the sweep of troops.

Before the generals could roll out any battle plans, the Aleppo sky lit up from multiple explosions, and the building that the rebels were gathered in began to crumble. The assembly broke up, and everyone ran for the exits.

Once outside, Mohammad sprinted down al-Khandaq Street, dodging hundreds of panicked and clueless residents, all desperate to know which way to go. Like them, he wasn't sure where to head, but he was determined not to sit by and do nothing. He bolted through side streets, hoping and praying to Allah that he would survive and find a way to help the rebels' cause.

Syrian soldiers combed the streets, searching door to door for the rebel terrorists who could be arrested or shot on sight. Mohammad scurried in and out of shadows, past block after block of abandoned apartments. Most residents had left as soon as the fighting closed in.

Stopping periodically in the darkness to avoid detection, he watched as a few remaining residents, obviously loyal to Assad, opened their doors and welcomed the soldiers. To Mohammad, they were traitors.

The city was home to large pockets of antigovernment terrorist groups, and for weeks rumors had circulated that doomsday from Bashar al-Assad was on its way. The explosions that night were part of an onslaught by Syrian helicopters that ultimately would drop barrel bombs on Aleppo by the end of 2016.

Random explosions spurred Mohammad on, and he was amazed that, almost with a sense of precognition, he had stayed clear of the blasts for a full half hour of running through the streets. Eventually, though, Mohammad feared there wasn't any safe place to hide. He paused, breathing hard, and leaned against the grimy wall of a gutted building. Movement and a muffled sound over his right shoulder caught his attention. The door to a basement had just been pulled shut from inside. Mohammad straightened, ran to the entrance, and twisted the door handle.

Great idea, he mused. *Hide in a ruined building. Assad's men won't waste bombs on a building that's already been destroyed.*

Eyes on the door to make sure he wasn't being followed, Mohammad backed down a set of creaking wooden steps. Suddenly he froze halfway down the dark flight of stairs, sensing that he was not alone. He pulled a pack of matches from his pants pocket, lit one, and turned toward the bottom of the passageway. The light of his flame reflected off several dozen terrified eyes.

A crowd of Muslim families filled the stairwell and the adjacent basement. Seeing Mohammad, they feared the worst, not knowing whose side it would be safe to be on if the intruder were an armed combatant. Whoever these people were—173 people in all—Mohammad decided in that instant that he needed friends, not enemies.

"Don't be alarmed. I'm with you." He raised his left hand in a conciliatory gesture.

The crowd made room for him, and Mohammad sat on the third step from the bottom of the stairwell. An idea formed as he studied the still-burning match in his right hand. With his left, he reached into his shirt pocket and extracted a cigarette from the day's pack. He touched the half-burned match to the cigarette and welcomed a moment of relaxation.

The newcomer and the basement refugees eyed one another in silence for more than a minute as Mohammad smoked. Then Mohammad finally took charge of the encounter.

"I know you're all afraid. But I am not! The Free Syrian Army will expel the vermin who have ruined our country. We are close!

"I was once a proud soldier in Bashar al-Assad's army. I imagined a day when Syria would control the entire Middle East and at last dispense the final misery on the despicable Jewish state. I love my country. I was born in Syria, and I will die in Syria."

He stood. From his basement-step podium, he would address this assembly as its leader.

"Yes, I was once loyal to Assad, but on March 15, 2011, I—we, many of us—found out what was really holding us back from once again becoming the great power of the Middle East. Bashar al-Assad was not our way ahead. He was our greatest obstacle.

"We in the army were not stupid, so I was not alone. *Sixty thousand* soldiers deserted him within a year. *Forty* generals left him, and they are now on our side. We. Will. Be. Victorious!"

At the word *victorious*, as if cued by a Syrian Arab Army (SAA) listening device in the basement, a shell from a T-73B3 Russian tank erupted overhead, and the remaining upper floors of the building began to collapse one by one. In unison, the basement crowd dove to the floor, and a hundred audible prayers begged for safety from being crushed.

Cowering on a lower step, Mohammad glanced up. The cement slab above them had held, but smoke and dirt choked the air, causing everyone to cough and gasp for oxygen. Mohammad and Abdul, another member of the Free Syrian Army, became the de facto leaders of the desperate assembly and quickly understood the precariousness of their situation. The building in which they were trapped lay at the heart of the battle zone as Assad's army had moved en masse to control the oldest section of the ancient city.

Where troops had swept the streets, snipers remained in place to eradicate any non-Alawite thing that moved.

Mohammad and Abdul wiped residue from a dirty window looking up to the street to see snipers atop adjacent buildings. For all they knew, one may have even been perched on what was left of the building they were in. Both men recognized that surviving the building collapse was a miracle, but they didn't know that it wouldn't be the last miracle they would witness in the coming week.

After a while Abdul assessed their situation. "The good news is that if the SAA saw anyone come into the basement, they'll think we're all dead." He pointed to the rear wall of the basement. "I also clawed through some of that rubble back there, and I believe we can scrape a way out. It'll take some hand digging, and we'll have to be very quiet. We don't dare tip off our 'supervisors' outside that there are survivors in the building. That would put a quick end to our stay here."

Mohammad shook his head. "We're doomed, Abdul. Who knows how long this building will stand? Still, the best thing we can do is not move, so we aren't shelled again. One more explosion, and we're permanently buried. Maybe the rest of the fighters will move on. Meanwhile, we've got food for a little while."

That first night the group had pooled what they'd managed to bring with them and assembled a larder of honey, falafel balls, pita bread, hummus, and even some baklava. If they ate sparingly, Mohammad estimated the food might last a week. Even more critical, though, drinkable water still flowed from the sink in the otherwise repulsive bathroom. The barely functioning toilet left the close quarters reeking of human waste.

Mohammad and Abdul did their best to keep morale up

and the group alive. Many could not bear the captivity, though, and they attempted to escape despite the leaders' urging to the contrary. A craving for fresh air overwhelmed most, and groups of two or three convinced themselves they could sneak out at night and escape. But each subsequent bid for freedom proved the insanity of trying. During the week, the group dwindled, leaving only those who did not attempt escape still alive in the basement. As Mohammad had warned would happen, no one made it out. Snipers, with orders to kill anything that moved, put down 157 of the basement dwellers.

When the food ran out at the end of day six, desperation deepened. The survivors rarely spoke.

Early on day seven Mohammad and Abdul sat, listless, on the bottom step of the stairwell. A clear but brief knock on their observation window at street level jolted the two men to attention. Everyone in the basement fell to the floor, trying to stay out of sight. If SAA soldiers had found the hiding place, everybody there would soon be dead.

Abdul inched his way up the concrete wall next to the window and peeked through the smudged glass. He flinched, then dropped to the ground and, eyes wide, spoke to Mohammad in a loud whisper.

"It's Him again!"

"What do you mean? *Who* again? A soldier?"

"Not a soldier. The Man in a white robe."

"Abdul, you're delirious!"

"No, Mohammad. I absolutely am not. He brought food to me when I was trapped in my office for a week last month."

"The same guy? This is the second time you've seen Him?"

"Yes—and more than that. But I'll tell you the story later.

Help me open the window." Abdul pointed overhead. "He has bread and water for us. *All* of us!"

Abdul and Mohammad stood up and saw that the window had already been opened from the outside. Bundles of food and jars of water sat within reach.

The Battle of Aleppo had lasted four interminable years as rebel fundamentalist Islamic groups like Jabhat al-Nusra and al-Qaeda, as well as the Free Syrian Army, dug in for the long haul. It became the longest military siege in modern history, and eventually the nightmare of "Syria's Stalingrad" eradicated a tenth of Aleppo's population.

As Abdul, Mohammad, and the survivors cowered in the basement, foreign-built tanks and armored personnel carriers swarmed the city. They controlled the roads while the Syrian Arab Air Force, aided by Vladimir Putin's contribution of the Russian air force, controlled the skies. Together they destroyed more than thirty thousand buildings.[6]

A few days later the siege finally ended in their quarter, and the snipers moved on to other assignments. Mohammad and Abdul helped fourteen survivors climb through the broken window that others had gone through to meet their deaths. Their basement duty fulfilled, the two ad hoc leaders walked a block through rubble, then paused to breathe in the outdoor air. Mohammad had been in that basement for ten days. Filthy but thankful to be alive, the two men stood in silence for several minutes before Abdul motioned for them to resume walking. Eyes on the ground, he spoke with conviction.

"Mohammad, that Man in the white robe who brought us bread and water . . . He was Jesus. You know this, don't you?"

Mohammad nodded slowly, stroking his chin with his left hand. "I do. He's been visiting me in dreams—even while we were holed up here. Abdul, why did we survive when so many died? Why *us*?"

Abdul didn't answer. Mohammad walked quietly for a half-dozen steps before continuing. "You know people will think we hallucinated if we talk about a Man in a white robe feeding us."

"But, Mohammad, how can they, when we have fourteen witnesses who saw Him too?"

"People won't believe us, Abdul. You know that."

Abdul nodded thoughtfully as the two men walked on in silence. They stopped at a corner they barely recognized as an intersection near the Aleppo National Museum. The routes to their respective families would take them in different directions from here. Their parting embrace was not a perfunctory Arab send-off but the fervent goodbye of two men bonded as brothers from the crucible they had survived.

Mohammad headed west toward Dina and their children, but he had one stop to make on the way. At the Armenian Evangelical Emmanuel Church, he paused to watch the Christians. What was left of the church roof rendered the structure unsafe, so several dozen believers knelt in worship on the sidewalk. Since they took little notice of Mohammad, he stepped quietly through the open front door and scanned the room.

He spotted what he was looking for on a dusty table. Mohammad Hadad stole a Bible, and then he left.

A CHANGE OF HEART

"Aisha, what's happening to me?" Dina stared at her parents' living-room floor but addressed her sister sitting at the other end of the sofa. "I find myself wondering about Mohammad."

"You mean like you actually care?"

Dina looked at Aisha and nodded. "It sounds strange, doesn't it? But yes."

Through the days of retreat with her parents, Dina had, story by story, shared with them the ghastly marriage she had endured since her wedding day. The only good part of the nightmare was the two children she adored. Even so, her parents were traditional Muslims and couldn't fathom the possibility that Dina might leave Mohammad, no matter how many other women she shared him with.

Dina could hardly imagine what her parents would think if they knew she had been praying for Mohammad's death in the war—and that if the fighting didn't do it, she would kill him herself. At this point, though, she doubted it would be up to her. She'd been with her parents for nearly two weeks, and even though the cease-fire was official now, Mohammad almost certainly hadn't lived long enough to see it.

Dina's mother seemed oblivious to concerns about Mohammad. Once the war's end was announced, she'd spent several days planning a celebration dinner for the family. Dina had helped by doing whatever her mother commanded, simply because she was glad to have something to occupy her time.

Dina, her children, her father and mother, and Aisha and her husband had settled at the dinner table for the celebration feast when a strong knock at the door startled them all. Still emotionally raw from the recent weeks of fighting, they eyed one another nervously.

After several seconds, Aisha nodded, pointed to herself, and slowly stood from the table. She crossed the living room and opened the front door. Gasping, she staggered back two paces.

Mohammad stepped into the room, looking first at Aisha, then at each family member in turn until his eyes met Dina's. He offered an uncharacteristically pleasant smile.

"*As-salaam-alaikum!*"[7]

No one spoke, but Maha and Jabar leaped from their chairs and ran to their father. Dina stood up at the table, her mind reeling over the unanticipated return of this tormentor. She slowly shuffled toward her husband.

Stopping an arm's length from him, she whispered, "I thought . . . I thought you were . . ."

"Dead? Is that what you thought? Is that what you hoped for, Dina?"

Smile gone, Mohammad sighed deeply before continuing. "For all I've put you through, Dina, I wouldn't blame you for thinking you'd be better off if I were dead. I guess I'm lucky you weren't hoping to kill me yourself."

Suddenly Mohammad's eyes smiled, and he laughed hard. Dina conjured a laugh in response and mused that she could win an Academy Award for Best Actress with this performance.

Mohammad reached for his wife's hand. "Dina, after we spend a few days with your family, let's go back home. Some of our neighborhood is in shambles, and there are still a few gun battles going on, but our apartment is intact. I checked on it before I came here." He paused, then eyed her softly. "I look forward to telling you my story."

Dina could not hide her disappointment and looked away. She had been free for eleven days from the man who had stolen her life, her joy, and all her hope. But she could not refuse to go with Mohammad, and it was understood that her family would not intervene. Dina would return to her torture chamber.

PRIVATE REVELATION

For the next few months Mohammad developed a method to hide his strange behavior from Dina. He could not let her know of his new activities until the time was right. So he waited each night for his wife to go to sleep. Once alone, he retrieved the stolen Bible from behind other books on the living-room shelf and read for several hours.

Although the Battle of Aleppo had ended, the war continued in other regions of Syria. Mohammad, though, gave little thought to the conflict and hoped his fundamentalist friends would assume he was dead. A new passion for the Man in the white robe consumed him. Every night he read his Bible, and most nights, dreams of Jesus kept his heart and mind at peace.

Although neither Dina nor the children knew the source, Mohammad shared his peace with the family. He no longer raised his voice for any reason, and he never beat Dina again.

Mohammad knew only one Christian in Aleppo, so on a warm morning in late spring, he headed for Nizar's home to tell him about the Jesus dreams. Although he had intended to stay for just an hour, he asked questions about Jesus and the Bible until the middle of the afternoon.

Nizar told Mohammad about a small church where other Muslims asked questions and shared similar experiences. He encouraged Mohammad to visit and assured the former FSA leader that everyone would respect his need for privacy. No one else would know he had come, and for the next six months, Mohammad never missed a meeting.

Meanwhile, Dina went to meetings of her own. Each week, she met Aisha and tried to put into words her confusion over Mohammad's strange—but welcome—new behavior. Aisha proposed theories. Mohammad was on drugs. Perhaps they'd even been prescribed to help him cope with post-traumatic stress disorder. Or, even more likely, he had taken up with another wife and was simply stepping out regularly to tend to her. Dina had no explanation herself but doubted each of Aisha's conjectures.

Toward the end of the year, Mohammad made his first attempt to alleviate Dina's confusion. After one of his Sunday outings, Mohammad walked quietly into the living room where Dina was reading.

"Dina," he said softly, "I need to tell you something."

Dina looked up from her book but said nothing. Then, for the first time in his marriage, Mohammad Hadad spoke to his wife from his heart.

"Dina, in the midst of war raging around us, a Man appeared to me many times in dreams. It was the same person every time, and I must tell you who it was." He paused. "The Man was Jesus. Once I began to read the Bible, I found it comforting beyond anything I've ever read. So I decided to take the next step.

"I visited a church. That's where I've been going on Sundays. And don't worry; I made sure no one saw me go.

"Dina, I heard words there like none I have ever heard in my life. They talked about Jesus forgiving me. Me! How could He do that? Anyone but me! My evil heart was so dark. I beat you mercilessly. I was rich but blew thousands of Syrian pounds buying women. I degraded you by bringing all those other women into my life, and I used to brag about it to you. Then I excused myself by quoting from the Qur'an to justify my . . . *sin*.

"But, Dina, Jesus saw right through me. When I read the Gospels and saw how He talked to men in the Bible called Pharisees, it was as if He was speaking to me alone." Mohammad shook his head and looked at the ceiling. "But why should that surprise me. After all, He visited me in dreams, and He *fed* us, Dina, when I was penned up in that basement for ten days. So after all of that, after reading the Bible for months, after being with true believers who follow Jesus with their whole hearts, I . . ."

His eyes remained locked on his wife. "Dina, I gave my life to Jesus. He has forgiven me."

Then for the first time in her marriage, Dina Hadad spoke from *her* heart to her husband. Her words were simple and clear: "I. Will. Never. Forgive. You."

The two eyed each other in silence for a full minute. Then Dina continued.

"Wow, Mohammad, you've done it this time. You're forgiven? How *convenient* is that?" She spat the words. "After all the misery you've caused me, I'm supposed to just look the other way? Never!"

Dina stood forcefully and brushed past Mohammad. Storming out of the house, this time Dina did the door slamming as she headed for Aisha's apartment.

THE VIGIL

For several weeks after Mohammad's confession of faith, Dina could no longer deny that her husband had changed for the better. No one could. Even Aisha, who hated her brother-in-law, admitted to Dina that he had never been so kind and hospitable.

The change in Mohammad stirred Dina's disillusionment with Islam, and she longed for the joy she now saw in her transformed husband. She could not escape one great fear, though, if she were to open herself to a similar experience. More than life itself, she wanted to never, ever forgive her husband. She could imagine doing anything but that. In fact, she relished having the upper hand and making Mohammad pay for the pain he'd caused her. Yet he persisted in wooing her toward his new way of life.

For eight months Mohammad invited Dina to church every Sunday, and each time she refused. One October morning, after she refused as usual, Mohammad went alone—again. But an hour after leaving home, Mohammad and his new friends sat on the floor, discussing chapter eight of the book of Romans, when a movement at the door caught his attention. He looked up and burst into tears.

All eyes turned toward Mohammad, and once they realized what had happened, his friends broke into applause and shouts of joy.

Dina Hadad had walked into the room.

IN PERSON WITH TOM AND JOANN

We met Dina and Mohammad on the coast of Lebanon to ask them questions about their relationship with each other and with

Jesus. We found them filled with joy—the bubbling-over, abiding kind of joy. Hours after we met them, their countenance had not changed. They were simply radiant.

Tom: Mohammad, how long did it take after Dina first came to the underground church before she gave her life to Jesus?

Mohammad: It was about four months, and then she was ready. But that first time I saw Dina walk slowly into the church was the most beautiful sight my eyes had ever seen. She had softened, and the love of Jesus was visible on her face.

How could I blame Dina for wanting to hang on to her hatred of me? I deserved it—all of it. I was the fundamentalist radical, but she was sick of our religion. I knew my words could not convince her about Jesus because she had seen me lie consistently for years. My whole life was a lie.

But then Jesus took over. I prayed that God would make me a good husband—a real husband like I read about in the New Testament, and He did that! I fell in love with Dina, and I wanted to tell her that I loved her, but I knew she could not receive those words—not yet. I even started to pray to Jesus before dinner. I would always thank Him for Dina and our two wonderful children.

It took Dina about a year before she found her way to Jesus—eight months of seeing what God was doing in my life and four months of coming to the underground church. When she received Jesus, it was a day I will never forget. She was finally free, and she also was able to forgive me. She loves Jesus with her whole heart and smiles all the time.

I think this is the way Dina and I will die. We expect to be killed because we love Jesus and left the religion of Islam. We expect to be martyrs for Jesus.

But Jesus has done so much for us. He forgave me for all my sins and my sickening life. He gave me a beautiful, loving wife in Dina, who also forgave me. Now we have a third child, and we tell each of our children every day about Jesus who set us free. How could we ever deny our Jesus?

Now Dina models Jesus for me. She amazes me. Dina has no fear and will do anything for Jesus. I'll give you an example.

One time, at the Zahle refugee camp in the Bekaa Valley of Lebanon, Dina knew she was being followed. The local "enforcers" were always after her, but by God's grace she managed to stay a half step ahead of them.

In the center of the disgusting camp and engulfed by the stench of a huge garbage dump there, she and eight other women hid behind a pile of trash as she told them her story. It was one of many times she met with Muslim refugees from her beloved Syria, but she had to make it quick because the fanatics had begun to suspect her.

That particular time, Dina told the women what she always tells them:

> It comes down to this, my dear ones: if you give your life to Jesus, your days may be short. I'm sure mine will be, but I gave up that concern months ago. Look at us. We have to hide just so I can read you a few verses from the Bible. If we did this out in the open, we'd be as dead as the donkey over there on that trash pile.
>
> But my life is beautiful because of Jesus. Even if I die today, I've had a full life, and it's all because of Him. This is what He wants to give you. I plead with you, my dear sisters. Jesus is waiting for you with open arms.

I interrupted the meeting that day because I knew her pursuers were likely getting close. She got my two-word text message: "Get out!"

But do you know what she did? My warrior-for-Christ wife simply bowed her head and prayed with those women. By the time they finished committing their lives to Jesus, they were all crying in joy—and Dina's cell phone was vibrating nonstop. I really wanted her out of there.

She told me later that the group didn't split up until they heard shouting from the fanatics within a stone's throw. They hugged, and once again, God was good to them. They all disappeared safely in different directions.

JoAnn: Dina, I know Jesus can do anything. Nothing is too hard for Him. But the continual beating . . . Mohammad was a terrorist right in your own home. And the sixty-six wives! You hoped to kill Mohammad. How did you ever manage to forgive him?

Dina: You see how amazing my husband is now. Thankfully, I was able to forgive Mohammad—but only because I experienced forgiveness first. In my own strength, I could not control the bitterness inside. I could not forgive him. Jesus gave me the power to forgive.

Before, if I'd had the chance, I could have killed Mohammad. Would I have actually done it? I don't know, but I sure wanted him dead. How sad is that? I wouldn't have been happy because my hatred of Mohammad had a grip on me, and seeing him dead would not have released it. But then Jesus broke through the hatred and took it away forever. This is the only way we can be free, and there are plenty of Muslim women who are as miserable as I was. I want to reach them and tell them Jesus is their solution.

Tom: Being with you both is like being with honeymooners. It's obvious you have a deep love for each other. Mohammad, when you walk by Dina, you kiss her on the top of her head or squeeze her hand. We're in Lebanon, and not much PDA—public display of affection—goes on here. But you don't care, do you?

Mohammad: Jesus came to me in dreams to prepare me for salvation. But He didn't visit Dina. Yet look at how He transformed her! She hated her life, and it was all because of me. I am madly in love with this woman of God. Look at the joy on her face.

JoAnn: Dina, you were not in the least bit attracted to your husband, were you?

Dina: Not at all. I was forced to marry him, and he made me sick. But when Jesus transformed him, the joy on his face and the kindness in his heart *made* him handsome. I still cannot believe he's the same man I once loathed.

JoAnn: Can you tell us about your third child? She arrived after both of you gave your lives to Jesus, correct?

Dina: She did! We wanted her name to tell what Jesus has done in our lives. Her name is *Shadi*, which in Arabic means "full of joy." She's our first child to grow up in our home after Jesus saved us.

JoAnn: Your name for your daughter is certainly anointed, for Shadi herself is full of joy and perpetual smiles!

Tom: You're in Lebanon now because you're refugees. Mohammad, you lost millions when your family took back your businesses to punish you for abandoning Islam. The sheikh who was closer than a brother has now called for your death in a *fatwa*.* Your parents also want you dead, and they've sent people to kill you. Are you afraid?

Mohammad: Refugee camps are where the radicals live and are, by far, the most dangerous places to share the gospel with Muslims. But Dina tells our story to anyone and everyone and gives Jesus the credit.

Even though our families want us dead—they say we have brought shame on them—Dina still calls them. They used to just hang up on her, but now she shares Jesus with them, and they are starting to listen. This is risky because they could easily find us. Her sister, Aisha, vowed to kill her even though she and Dina were so close. Our parents have plenty of friends living in Lebanon that they could send to kill us.

In Lebanon, there are between one and two million Syrian refugees. Dina wants every woman to hear about Jesus so they can reach their families. I watch her and marvel at what Jesus has done. She has a fire in her heart to touch Muslim women for our Savior.

JoAnn: What words do you want to leave with the new friends reading your Jesus story?

Dina: I was probably in worse shape emotionally, physically, and spiritually than Mohammad because of the hatred embedded so deeply in my heart. When I did forgive Mohammad, it broke the stronghold of revenge that held me captive. Right after that, Mohammad told me that he loved me. He had never said those words to me before. In fact, he said over and over that he loves me. We were both finally free. We hugged, and we kissed, and it was truly wonderful.

He told me these words I will never forget: "Dina, I love you, and I will always love you until the day I die. And I promise to love *only* you."

So, you see, we have all we need in this life. We have Jesus, we have a loving marriage, and we have three beautiful children who love Jesus too.

There are two important lessons I have learned in my life since coming to faith in Christ:

1. Jesus forgave me of my sins, which were many.
   So how could I withhold forgiveness from others, including my husband? People hear my story, and they cannot believe that I forgave Mohammad and am still married to him. But they just don't know the incredible power of Jesus' forgiveness.
   I realized hate held me captive and permeated every fiber of my being. Until I laid it at the feet of Jesus, I was its prisoner. I seethed in hate and anger

at Mohammad's joy and kindness. As much as I longed for what he had, invisible iron bars held me in bondage. It wasn't until Jesus opened my eyes to the ugliness of my own dark sins, as well as my need for repentance, that He washed me clean. For the first time in my life, I felt whole, pure, and forgiven. Joy took up residence in my heart that day and has been a constant companion ever since. With forgiveness as an intentional choice, joy is a natural by-product.

He wants to do the same for you. Will you let Him? What injustice in your life is holding you captive? Forgiveness is a vehicle that transports you to the place of joy.

2. As Christians, we believe Jesus performs life-changing miracles.

We pray for miracles, but do I *expect* miracles? Do you? That's a question we should ask ourselves daily. We should *expect* miracles because Jesus told us to ask for them. When our lives were in shambles and war was raging around us, evil was everywhere. Mohammad was ready to die for an unworthy cause he believed in, and I was willing to stoop so low as to take my husband's life.

In the black darkness of sin, the light of Jesus illuminates brightly, and miracles are God's way of opening our eyes to His salvation for lost souls. But when life becomes ordinary, when we have the truth of God's Word and are walking in His precepts, do we continue to look for and seek His miracle-working power? If not for ourselves, then how about when we are seeking to share the good news of the gospel with those who have not yet given their lives to Christ?

That is where my beloved husband and I now see miracles. We continue to pray for the day when all of our family members will give their lives to our Savior.

Also, please pray for us. Syria is a dangerous place, but we want to go back at the first chance. Hatred there is rampant. No wonder our war drags on. The religion we came from seeks revenge, and the Middle East is filled with violent ethnic-religious wars. We also know, because we now follow Jesus, people would line up to kill us.

I used to laugh at Christians. Then I saw the pictures of Syrian believers willing to die on a cross for their faith in Jesus. But I wasn't willing to die. I was ready to kill.

On His last night of life on earth, Jesus said, "Greater love has no one than this: to lay down one's life for one's friends" (John 15:13).

Now I understand those words, and I embrace them. If I am privileged to go back to Syria, I'm willing to give up my life for Jesus. And if that is God's plan for me, I know my loving husband will be right by my side.

---

*A *fatwa* is a legal ruling given by a Muslim cleric—including a decree that one who has left the Islamic faith is subject to execution.

As for me, I would seek God,
>   and to God would I commit my cause,
who does great things and unsearchable,
>   marvelous things without number: . . .
he sets on high those who are lowly,
>   and those who mourn are lifted to safety.

>   —Job 5:8–9, 11 esv

CHAPTER 3

"MARRY HIM, OR YOUR MOTHER DIES!"

Farah Abbas staggered back three steps, ears ringing from the full-hand slap to her right cheek. Her father's arm felt as strong as ever.

"So this is how I celebrate my wedding? The handprint on my face will go well with my dress!"

Nabeel Abbas sneered at his only daughter, then stormed toward the bedroom door, hissing profanities at the female offspring he merely tolerated.

"It's no wedding dress anyway," Farah shouted as her father retreated. "It's a dress of *shame*!"

Stunned by her words, the man stopped and turned to Farah for an instant, his face contorted in disgust. The freedom he had allowed his once submissive daughter had changed her into an all-too-modern woman. She needed a marriage to put her back in her place. He slammed the door as he left and did not look at his daughter until her wedding day three days later.

ONE MONTH EARLIER

Nearly a quarter of Jordan's residents were now refugees since the war in Syria began in 2011. The Hashemite economy reeled under the weight of the human catastrophe across the border, barely providing subsistence to more than one million Syrian indigents.[1] The only things rising faster than the number of people relocating to UNRWA[2] camps were inflation and the jobless rate.

Unemployment and the scarcity of money it brought assured many long workdays for loan officers at the Central Bank of Jordan. Despite the early afternoon announcement that only half of the customers waiting to see someone about mortgage relief would be served before the bank's three o'clock closing time, no one left.

Two hours after closing time, Farah was still listening to yet another sob story from a family on the brink of collapse. She gazed past the man pleading with her and through the window visible over his shoulder.

On top of a hill just a few hundred meters in that direction stood the Citadel of Amman. Its massive cut stones—some more than thirty centuries old—looked down on the city of her birth. She wondered how much longer her country could survive in these circumstances. *Certainly not three thousand years.* Farah shook her head to clear the thought from her mind and refocused on the man's story. On some days she was not so much a loan officer as a counselor.

She startled at the ring of her phone and was immediately thankful for the interruption it offered. Even better was the voice she heard. It was Rania, her best friend and one of the bank's tellers, still at work.

"They're here again, Farah, staring at you and making the usual obscene comments. Our 'disgusting customers' are back and headed your way." Rania paused. "They make me sick."

Farah merely nodded and hung up the phone. She stood abruptly, held up her index finger to the man whose story had been interrupted by the call, and left her desk without a word. She heard the man at her desk sigh mournfully as she headed for the break room.

Farah, too, moaned as she trotted to a safe haven. Planting herself beside the NESCAFÉ 3in1 coffee display, she fumed over the men she knew by now were standing at her desk.

"Not in a million years would I be caught dead with either of those despicable goons masquerading as human beings," she ranted to the empty break room. "They actually think I would come to one of their 'parties.' Every girl in Amman knows to stay away from them."

Ten minutes later, the goons had left, and Farah walked back to her desk. As she sat down to resume her meeting with the desperate customer, Farah noticed a handwritten note tucked under her coffee cup. Without reading it, she opened a drawer and shoved the message into her desk.

An hour later, when the bank had finally closed, Rania counted the money in her cash drawer and headed for Farah's cubicle.

"I saw Jamal leave a note on your desk. Did you read it? Please tell me you threw it in the garbage can."

"Rania, believe me, I wanted to trash the note, but I'm saving it as evidence for when I slap his face. That way, when the boss wants to fire me for offending a customer, I can show him how vile these men really are. Jamal and Mustafa Samaha have sex overload on the brain. Jamal should be arrested for what he wrote in that last pornographic message. I hate both brothers, but especially Jamal." Farah paused in thought. "What's the nickname his brother always calls him?"

Rania smirked. "You mean 'monster'?"

Farah nodded, then shook her head.

"Good night, Rania! See you at Friday prayers tomorrow. I just hope we don't run into you-know-who." She rolled her eyes. "As if Allah would ever listen to Jamal's empty words."

PRIDE BEFORE THE FALL

The next day, just outside the parliament building on King al-Hussein Street, Farah stopped to admire the graceful blue dome of the King Abdullah I Mosque, then glanced at her watch. Eleven thirty in the morning. She still had thirty minutes before the start of midday prayers, so she lingered, taking in the beautiful sight. Other than being a regular at Friday prayers, Farah wasn't religious, but she was a Jordanian through and through—which meant she overflowed with pride for the stunning building.

Minutes later, as Farah walked through the angular gateway to Jordan's most famous Muslim place of prayer, she felt deeply satisfied at *her* accomplishments, even though they had nothing to do with Islam. She was single, successful, and in command of her own life. Although, at twenty-six, she lived with her parents, they let her come and go as she pleased and were blessedly moderate by Islamic standards. Farah thought of herself as a "progressive Muslim." To her parents, though, that just meant she wasn't serious about her faith—and they were right.

Attending Friday prayers was good for business. Farah cared little for either the prayers or the imam's sermons. She used the time for a mental review of her calendar—appointments with customers who mattered and her social activities in the upcoming week. Being at the mosque was also good for her favorite pastime. It allowed her brain space to focus on what she would buy on her next shopping spree.

She looked around, noting that Rania apparently would be a no-show once again. As Farah headed toward the women's prayer section, she saw her father scurry in at the last minute. He had become a regular ever since Farah's mother was diagnosed with breast cancer. Nabeel carried the crushing weight of Safiyyah's condition everywhere he went. Farah saw it in his slumped shoulders, the desperation on his face, and the fact that he brushed past his daughter without even noticing her.

Seeing her father was a painful reminder of her mother's sickness. Business and shopping would not heal her. But could prayers? Farah paused in thought at the entrance to the women's section. Stepping slowly into the open space, she decided to pray this week.

By the next day at the TAJ mall, Farah had forgotten her fleeting encounter with faith. A hot spot for upper-middle-class Jordanians, the mall occupied most of Farah's Saturdays. Typically, she roamed from one store to another, adoring the lavish opportunities to add clothes and accessories to her accumulation of current fashions. This week, though, Rania joined her, and as always with her favorite coworker, that meant serious shoe shopping.

"Rania, I can enjoy myself today because my mother was actually feeling better last night. Now that the surgery is done, her doctors say, with chemo and radiation, she should be fine. So let's celebrate the good news." She grinned and linked arms with her friend at her left elbow. "Today, no less than three pairs of shoes each!"

Farah pulled Rania past the Calvin Klein Jeans store, and the two women headed for ALDO Shoes. They acted more like sisters than friends and looked as if they could be models on a Jordanian tourism brochure. The PR lords of the Hashemite Kingdom, of course, wanted exactly such an image presented to the West—young, pretty, successful Jordanian women living free and enjoying an outing in one of the Middle East's hippest malls. But despite designer hijabs, the look belied a dark underbelly even the most affluent women could not escape.

The next week Farah again joined Rania at the TAJ mall. But before the two made it to a single one of the mall's half-dozen shoe stores, a phone call from Farah's father signaled that her perfect life was about to unravel.

She accepted the call, knowing it would not be pleasant. Nabeel was breathing as heavily as if he'd just sprinted a mile.

"What's the matter, Father? Why are you crying?"

Between breaths he told Farah the unbelievable news: "Your mother's doctors just confirmed that her cancer is back, and it's spreading. The initial numbers looked good, but after further testing, the oncologist did a CAT scan on an area that concerned him." Nabeel paused, hardly able to speak. "He found another mass. Farah, if he hadn't done the scan, your mother probably would've died before we had a chance to do anything about it.

"Our hearts are breaking. We must do something. Your mother needs surgery within ten days."

Farah felt as if she had been hit by a car. She slumped against a pillar in the food court, where she had stopped to take the call. She slid slowly to the floor.

As Farah sat there on the floor of the mall, tears dripped down her cheeks while her father explained his plan to save her mother.

"Farah, I wanted to do this in person. I'm sorry for telling you this on the phone . . . I hope you are with Rania." He took a deep breath. "We need the money from your account that the government has been holding back until you're married. I've checked, and it's up to 2,000 JDs.[3] That's not bad for eight years of work!"

Farah spoke robotically, fearing her father's response. "But I'm not planning to get married anytime soon, Father. How can you access the money?"

"Farah, I've arranged for a marriage. Your mother and I have already talked this out. He's a good man, just a little older, and he's coming to see you tonight." Nabeel's words were decisive. "He looks forward to meeting you."

"*Baba*, no!"[4] Farah said it so loudly that several passersby looked down at the crying woman. "Please, let's talk about this! I'm a modern woman. I get to pick the man I marry. This is so wrong. I cannot do this!"

Nabeel said nothing for several seconds, then spoke coldly. "Farah, we are observant Muslims. This is what we do. Your mother and I pick the groom because we know what is best for you. This is an emergency. You will learn to love him."

Nabeel paused long enough that Farah opened her mouth to respond, but he cut her off. "Let me put it this way: *marry him, or your mother dies!* The man's name is Jihad, and he will be here at seven tonight. Don't be late."

Farah clicked off the call and stared blankly past a dozen vinyl chairs at the McDonald's on the other side of the food court. For an hour Farah and Rania sat on the floor, talking and crying as shoppers walked around them.

"Rania, should I just run away and never contact my parents again?"

"If you do that, Farah, your mother will die." Rania stared at the floor and shook her head. "That's not a solution."

Farah pressed her head against the pillar and looked at the ceiling. "His name is Jihad . . . Gee, I wonder if he's a fundamentalist? Ha!" Farah's laugh disintegrated into sobs as she tried to fathom the horror of this turn in her life.

The two women sat in silence for several minutes. Finally Rania reached for Farah's hand. The friends stood slowly and began a somber walk to the mall exit. After tearfully hugging Rania in the parking lot, Farah headed home to face the brutal reality of her predicament.

Farah tried not to cry as her mother hugged her at the front door and thanked her for funding the surgery. As heartbroken as she felt, withholding tears was easy compared to facing her father. She did not look at Nabeel but stepped past him toward her bedroom. Safiyyah followed Farah and spoke softly as the two reached the door at the top of the stairs.

"I realize you don't know him, Farah, and that marrying now

is not what you wanted, but Allah is in charge of these things. He knows best. He has allowed it." She glanced downstairs, then back at Farah. "I didn't know your father, either."

"But, Mother, your marriage to Father has been terrible!" Farah turned and pointed at the older woman. "You said it yourself."

"It was, for many years." Safiyyah nodded. "But your father no longer beats me."

Farah rolled her eyes in disgust. "Are you trying to say this wedding for me is a good thing? Listen to yourself, Mother, and how you've settled for this dismal marriage of yours. He may not beat you, but he screams at you every day."

Safiyyah looked at her daughter sadly, then turned and walked silently out of the bedroom.

Farah lay alone on her bed, thoughts buffeting her mind:

Maybe it won't be so bad.

I wish it could be someone like Wael from ALDO. He's so nice— and so handsome!

Who am I kidding? He'll probably be as old as Father.

Two hours later she startled at the sound of the doorbell. Seven o'clock, exactly as planned. Her stomach knotted. This was the day—the hour!—Farah had sworn would never come. That the choice of her future husband had been decided without her consent was unfathomable.

Farah rose to a sitting position and stared for several seconds at the bedroom door. She decided to sneak a peek at the man who would be her groom, so she stepped to the door and twisted her head to look down the stairway without being seen.

"No!" The word escaped involuntarily, audible by anyone in the house. She clasped a hand over her mouth, squeezed her eyes shut, and pressed her back into the doorway as if it could save her from an unthinkable fate.

Jamal Samaha was standing in the living room.

MEET AND GREET

Nabeel jabbered gleefully, just as he did when he gushed about Jordan's King Abdullah.

"Farah! Jihad is here. He's *very* excited to see you."

Nabeel and Safiyyah Abbas stood together, beaming, and watched Farah's reaction as she bounded down the steps.

"Jihad just told me that you two have met before." Nabeel welcomed his daughter with raised arms. "I had no idea. What a coincidence! Another thing I learned is that Jihad is a nickname. His real name is Jamal."

Nothing could have prepared the parents for what happened next.

Eyes brimming with angry tears, Farah balled her right hand into a fist, walked wordlessly up to Jamal, and with all her strength, punched him in the nose. The man reeled backward and sat involuntarily on the living-room couch.

"I don't care how much Mother needs surgery. I cannot marry this sick man, Father." She turned toward her parents while pointing at Jamal with the hand that had struck him. "He stalks me at work. This is utterly humiliating! Can't you find someone else? Anybody!"

She glared at Jamal, then back at her parents. "The last time he was in the bank, he wrote a note so foul that if I let you read it, you'd throw him out of our house for good. Baba, listen to me. Please!"

Nabeel's eyes bulged. Farah thought he looked as if his head might explode. He glared at Farah, then looked past her and apologized obsequiously to the bleeding man on the couch.

Jamal had pulled a handkerchief from his pocket and was squeezing his nose to stop the flow of blood. He stood slowly and smiled unconvincingly at his bride-to-be.

"Why, Farah, I didn't mean anything by that harmless little note. I was just . . . just confessing my love for you."

Farah narrowed her eyes, rejecting Jamal's spurious story. "Jamal, that was sexual harassment, not a love letter. Or don't you know the difference?" She flicked her hand in his direction. "I'd sign a restraining order against you but never a marriage contract!"

Nabeel Abbas's patience had worn out. He laid into Farah as he often did with his wife, screaming so loudly that Safiyyah ran to shut the windows so their neighbors wouldn't hear the details of his latest explosion.

Fifteen minutes later Jamal had left the family to its standoff, but Nabeel seemed only to be getting started when Farah raised the palms of her hands toward her father and spoke to her mother.

"I want to help, Momma. I really do. I'll agree to a marriage but not to Jamal! No way!"

"You *will* marry Jamal!" Nabeel turned as if to walk away, then spun quickly toward his daughter. To make his one last point, he leaned so close to Farah that she could feel his breath on her face. His wagging index finger nearly touched the woman's left cheek.

"The wedding is in three days!"

Farah pushed past her father and ran up the stairs to her room, wailing as if a death in the family had just occurred. As far as she was concerned, it might as well have been her death.

Thirty minutes later Nabeel threw open Farah's bedroom door and tossed a wedding dress on her bed. Then he walked slowly toward his daughter, eyes riveted on her face. Farah sensed what was coming next. She'd witnessed this scene before.

Nabeel slapped her face with such force, it knocked her back three steps.

"So this is how I celebrate my wedding? The handprint on my face will go well with my dress! It's no wedding dress anyway. It's a dress of *shame*."

Satisfied with the damage done to his daughter, Nabeel stormed out of the room while Farah's rant continued.

"Not that it's going to be a real wedding anyway." She stuck her head out the bedroom door and shrieked at the open space above the stairs. "I hate this man I have to marry!"

Everyone in the house heard. But no one listened.

Until nearly midnight Farah sat on the floor of the bedroom and talked to herself.

"I'm mad at everyone in my life! Even the king of Jordan for the stupid rule our government put in place to 'help' single women. But it's blackmail, I tell you."

The dress Nabeel had brought didn't fit, but because Farah refused to leave the house for the next twenty-four hours, her parents brought dresses from the Elite Bridal Shop so she could try them on in private.

MARRIED AND MISERABLE

To Farah, her life became a complete disaster the day she was forced to marry Jamal Samaha. Her dreams of freedom to find real love with a man of her choosing became a nightmare of sub-jection to Jamal's cruel domination. Not even the knowledge that her marriage had likely saved her mother's life could compensate for the grim reality she now endured.

The man's sick control began on the first day of their honey-moon. Jamal told Farah she could no longer work because he wanted to have children immediately, and when the new bride suggested she might work until she got pregnant, his only answer was a fist to her face. The brutal first day was merely the begin-ning of a dismal honeymoon week. The groom abused his new wife for seven full days.

Jamal's insistence on getting Farah pregnant as soon as possible was a key to his strategy of domination. He knew that Farah would never try to leave him if they had children. In Islamic culture the father always gets the sons and daughters in a divorce, and most any woman will endure a husband's abuse rather than abandon her children.

Upon returning to Amman from the week of honeymoon torture in Aqaba, Farah mustered the courage to ask again if she could continue working at the job she loved—at least in the short term. This time Jamal simply laughed and explained that he had already talked to her boss and resigned for her. From then on the weight of Jamal's control crushed the life out of Farah's spirit.

Within the first year of their marriage, Jamal had his way: Farah was pregnant. The man gloated mightily in front of his friends over the news that the baby was a boy—then even more so two years later when Farah bore their second son.

Farah became a mere tool for growing their family. Jamal lavished love and attention on his sons but offered his wife only disdain and abuse. Yet every night Jamal insisted on the same routine: dinner, then the bedroom. Farah was left only to daydream about being loved, and she fantasized about how beautiful her life could have been if she had said yes to just one of the men who so often asked her out to dinner or a movie when she worked at the Bank of Jordan.

HIS HAPPINESS, HER HUMILIATION

One Friday after Jummah, Farah stopped at the market to buy food for that evening's meal. A stark, black hijab had replaced the colorful designer styles she and Rania had worn. Now an observant Muslim at the command of her husband, she was no longer the girl who was free to do whatever she pleased—or the progressive Muslim woman with a successful career.

Tucking Mahmoud and Medo into the grocery cart, Farah hauled her two sons and her own dispirited body through the store. Several passing moms told her how cute the boys were, and the taste of appreciation from other human beings was the highlight of her day.

Passing a mirror in the cosmetic section, Farah was shocked at her reflection. How she had aged! And there was no hiding the sadness in her eyes. She was a shattered woman without hope.

Staring at the despairing image, she muttered, "I don't think I can go any lower."

Suddenly she shook her head, looked at her watch, and panicked. She had only an hour and a half to get home, make dinner, and brace herself for Jamal's arrival.

"You consider this slop of a meal fit for a man?" Jamal shouted as he threw his dinner—plate and all—in the trash can. "It's disgusting . . . almost as disgusting as you are!"

He swung an open hand at Farah, slapping her hard across the face. Tears and shame filled her eyes. A swollen cheek and a bruise would follow. Again.

After Jamal had retreated to the living room, Farah fished the chipped dinnerware out of the trash and began cleaning up the remains of a dinner she had worked hard to prepare. Once again she wondered where she had missed the mark. It seemed she always did *something* wrong, no matter how hard she tried to get things right.

I followed his mother's recipe exactly as she instructed. Jamal raved about this dish when we had dinner with his family last week. What did I do wrong this time?

Farah planned her meals specifically to please her husband, not because she cared about him but to spare herself from his swinging fists. Part of her heart died each time he treated her like a worthless possession, yet she knew that if she left him, he would have sole custody of the children.

The heartbreak was even worse each time Jamal hit one of their sons for no apparent reason. Fearing a brutal greeting, five-year-old Mahmoud hid each time he heard his father coming home from work. Three-year-old Medo simply clung to the back of his mother's legs to stay out of his father's way. It seemed to Farah that when Jamal wasn't hitting one of them, he was shouting at them. For all three, the best times of day were when Jamal was away from home—at work, visiting friends, or seeing his extended family.

The morning after the latest postdinner beating, Farah

adjusted her hijab to cover a bruised cheek. She had become a master at hiding evidence of Jamal's cruelty. Yet despite the pain of lumps and bruises, the emotional agony was even harder to endure.

She was relieved when Jamal left early for work, simply because it meant he would be gone longer than usual. More time apart should have given her a small measure of peace, but it didn't. The ache in her heart denied any feelings of happiness or joy, even during times of relief when Jamal was absent.

She often wished Jamal's disapproval would motivate him to divorce her. She would be free of him, but concern for her sons always stopped short her longing for a separation. What would become of Medo and Mahmoud in Jamal's sole custody? At other times she simply wished to die. She would be free of this controlling freak of nature, but that, too, would leave her precious sons at risk.

Shame, loneliness, sadness, and depression morphed into self-loathing. Farah ached for something to fill the gaping hole in her heart. Although she cried out to Allah to rescue her from the debilitating depression, night after night, he remained silent—distant, remote—and her tears were wasted once again.

BETTER OFF THAN A SYRIAN REFUGEE?

Farah eventually resigned herself to the disaster that was her life and one day realized she had been keeping her stylish career clothing for no good reason. The pieces had represented a hope for redemption—but now she knew it would never come. So to confirm acceptance of her terrible reality, she decided to give to the Syrian refugees the clothes she wore when she worked at the bank. Perhaps her fashions could bring joy to someone else's desperate life.

Amman's Alliance Church sponsored an ongoing clothing drive, and when Farah arrived to donate her wardrobe, she found the small church building jammed with Syrians. Outside, a long line of more refugees waited to get in.

Something bothered Farah about the scene, and she set down her bag of clothing just inside the church entrance. When she paused to think, the dissonance she felt formed a series of questions in her mind: *Why is it that Muslims are not helping their fellow Muslims, and I have to go to a* church *to help refugees? Why not the mosque? Are we letting the Christians do our job now?*

A new sensation cut short Farah's musing. It was the rank odor of the Syrian women whose *abayas* should have been washed weeks ago.[5] Farah curled her lip involuntarily at the stench as she scanned piles of goods donated by Jordanians—clothes, shoes, even kitchenware.

Misery loves company, I guess. She picked up her bag of clothing. *These helpless victims are even worse off than I am.*

As Farah jostled into the crowded space, refugee smiles greeted her. She stopped, again shocked by an observation: *These women are happy!* For many, she knew, their husbands were dead. None had money, and their children were all dressed in wretchedly dirty clothes. Yet many were laughing as if having the time of their lives. How could this be?

Farah stared at the throng of women, trying to believe what she was seeing. Thoughts spun through her brain: *Refugees are nothing more than a number once they cross the border and leave Syria. They've lost homes, family members, and their identities. Whatever they've gained in life has been taken away, and they've had to start over, dirt poor. Yet look at them!* Then the most poignant observation of all shot through Farah like a jolt of electricity: *So why am I sadder than they are?*

For several seconds Farah's eyes roamed the room. She had to know why the women surrounding her were so upbeat and decided instantly that she would find out. She chose a smiling woman sifting through a nearby pile of dresses, walked up to her, and spoke abruptly.

"What's your name?"

Startled by the interruption in her search for the right size dress, the woman looked Farah in the eye and answered warmly, "My name is Ekram, and I'm from Deir ez-Zor."

She waved her hand toward three children pawing through a pile of clothing behind her. "And these are my children."

Farah frowned. "Deir ez-Zor? The Islamic State controlled your city during the most intense fighting in the civil war. How can you possibly . . ."

"Have a smile on my face?" Ekram finished the question. "I lost family and saw things I did not think humans could do to one another. My husband was killed because he would not join the terrorist machine that almost destroyed our entire country.

"But the Islamic State made me reconsider my life and my religion. This was not true Islam—at least not what I'd been taught. So you want to know why I smile?" Ekram's eyes sparkled playfully. "It's a secret. If you come back tomorrow, I'll tell you!"

Puzzled, Farah cocked her head. "A secret?" She eyed Ekram for several seconds. "Are you on drugs?"

Ekram giggled and shook her head. "Come back tomorrow, and you'll find out."

Once back at her apartment, with Mahmoud and Medo napping, Farah called Rania. After explaining her decision to give away the clothes that the two of them had spent so many hours shopping for, Farah rattled off her amazing observations from the morning at the Christian church.

"Rania, the Syrian refugees I met today smiled more than Jordanians! What is their problem? Many of them lost their husbands." She chuckled. "Although I can say that would certainly make *me* smile, that's beside the point. I don't understand them. What in the world could it be?"

Rania thought for a few seconds before answering. "Maybe they've found some sort of true contentment, and it gives them a sense of peace. Or maybe they just love being in Jordan. I don't know. Why don't you ask *them?*"

"I guess I will. I'm going to the church tomorrow afternoon at one o'clock to meet with several of the women there." Farah paused. "Please come with me, Rania. I hardly ever get to see you anymore. I don't blame you for not wanting to visit me at my apartment because of Jamal. But you've got to meet these women. It's important. I feel it."

"Okay, Farah. I'll go with you, but I've got to get off the phone now. The boss is looking at me—and he's angry."

MUSLIM WOMEN IN A CHRISTIAN CHURCH

As Farah and Rania rounded Third Circle and headed toward Second, Rania pressed her right hand onto her friend's arm.

"Farah, I don't feel good about this. We are *Muslims* going to a *church*. Doesn't that send up any red flags with you? What's more: it's Friday, and we should be going to the mosque."

Farah stopped walking and laughed.

"Like you *ever* go to the mosque anymore, Rania!" She cocked her head at her bestie. "Why be uptight about meeting someone at a church? Religion doesn't mean anything to you— and it never has." Farah shook her head. "Besides, it's where I met Ekram when she was getting her handout."

Rania rolled her eyes, looked at Farah, rolled them again, then scrunched her face at her friend. "Fine, but let's make it quick. What if my family saw me at the church?"

Farah couldn't resist. "What if your family saw you at the mosque? I think they'd be more stunned to see you *there!*"

Five women, eyes sparkling and heads swathed in dusty hijabs, stood on their tiptoes, peeking over the church fence as Rania and Farah approached the front gate. The two friends were still squabbling about the visit to a Christian place.

"Farah!" Ekram yelled loud enough to stop the conversation. "Over here!"

The pair entered the church courtyard and skirted the fence to where Ekram and her friends waited. Ekram motioned them toward six plastic stools surrounding a matching table, set with tea and sweets. Then the hostess stepped to another table nearby and pulled an empty chair to the meeting space. All seven women sat down.

Farah spoke first. "This is my friend Rania. Ekram, who are your friends?"

Ekram beamed. "Actually, we're all from different cities

in Syria. It took us coming to Jordan to meet. We were drawn together because of our backgrounds."

Rania jumped in. "Suffering can bring people together, can't it?"

"Well, it can, but that's not what connected us. We know that God brought us together." She paused and looked Farah and Rania each in the eye. "This may end our conversation, if you take this the wrong way, but . . . well, here goes.

"Jesus came to each of us in our dreams when we lived in Syria. We saw Him many times. He also told each one of us to leave our country and go to Jordan. For me, Jesus dreams came every night as I walked with my family toward the border. We were on the road many days. I know you'll have trouble believing this, but each night Jesus would come and tell me what to do the next day.

"He guided me and my children through all the danger. I didn't know which way was safe or how to avoid Jabhat al-Nusra or ISIS. How could I keep from being taken as another wife, and how could I keep my children from becoming orphans?"

Ekram pointed to the other four women as she continued. "My friends here had similar experiences with Jesus. We are all widows because we lost our husbands in the war. But Jesus guided us. He was our GPS."

Ekram's friends laughed.

Farah and Rania each took a long drink of tea and sat quietly. They glanced at each other, disbelief in their eyes. Finally Farah spoke.

"But you are Muslims! You're dressed like Muslims." Then she added feebly, "Jesus is for Christians."

Ekram stood up, mulling over how to respond. "That's what

we thought too. Our imams told us that, of course. But now we know we've been deceived our whole lives.

"The reason I smile . . . the reason we all do . . . is simple: we've given our lives to Jesus." Ekram let out a breath. "There. I said it! I'm sure you've never heard that before from five women who *were* Muslims.

"We are MBBs—Muslim-background believers. And Jesus is our Savior. Now we follow Him—and love Him. *That* is why we have joy. It comes from Him, not from our circumstances." Ekram shook her head emphatically. "We're no longer Muslims."

Rania and Farah simply stared in response. They looked slowly from Ekram to each of the other women in turn.

"Refugees have no rights," Ekram began again, "and we can't go back to our homes in Syria. They aren't there anymore, and besides, we have no husbands. Who would protect us? No one wants us." Ekram pointed her index finger toward the sky. "But Jesus does."

Farah was transfixed and wanted to hear more. Rania, on the other hand, couldn't leave soon enough. Sensing Rania's turmoil, Farah pointed at the gate through which they had entered.

"Rania, if you need to go, I understand. I'm staying a little longer, though."

Three hours after Rania left, Farah headed for home. The small New Testament she smuggled in the pocket of her abaya fit nicely under a stack of hand towels in the kitchen. She figured it was safe there from Jamal since he never lifted a finger in the "woman's workplace." After meeting all of Jamal's demands that evening, Farah stayed up late and wrote several dozen questions she wanted to ask Ekram.

At their meeting the next day, the women answered every question to Farah's satisfaction. She cautiously began to hope that Ekram and her friends really had something special to offer her. That evening, she even smiled at Jamal and was astounded when he didn't throw his dinner in the trash.

The next week Ekram and the other Syrian ladies prayed with Farah as she gave her life to Christ. They stood from the plastic chairs around what had become their conference table and hugged, the six women weeping together. Farah felt the emptiness and pain in her heart swept away by peace and inexplicable joy. She began smiling.

THE MEETING AFTER THE MEETING

Farah's heart still brimmed with joy and gratitude by the time Jamal and the boys were asleep. She retrieved her New Testament from among the hand towels, opened to the gospel of John, and read from the first chapter: "But to all who did receive him, who believed in his name, he gave the right to become children of God" (v. 12 ESV).

Farah laughed out loud, then quickly prayed that her outburst wouldn't wake Jamal.

"I am now . . . a child of God."

She quietly repeated the words again and again as she stashed the precious book back in its hiding place and returned to her bedroom. The idea was too hard to fathom. She slipped into bed and faded to sleep with a smile on her face and the comforting truth resonating in her heart: *I am a child of God!*

Someone or something ushered Farah into an immense,

brightly lit room. The light was intense yet not painful, and the sound from a multitude of voices tickled her ears. Despite the volume, the noise was pleasant. Charming laughter punctuated a chorus of high-spirited conversations.

As she adjusted to the surroundings, a profusion of colorful women's clothing tantalized her chocolate-brown eyes, and the sweet scent of flowers blended with tempting hints of a delicious meal yet to be served. Farah's stomach rumbled.

To her left, Farah saw a sweeping spiral staircase beckoning her to ascend. As she climbed the steps, the beauty around her slowly dissolved, leaving a sole figure standing before her. A Man in a dazzling white robe was watching her, His garment flowing regally to His feet.

Farah's eyes drifted slowly up the length of the elegant figure and stopped at His exquisite face. She had never seen—or felt— the all-consuming love that emanated from this otherworldly Person. His eyes reached into the core of her soul; yet, at the same time, the look felt as gentle as a summer breeze.

Farah's fear and shame evaporated in the intensity of His perfect love, and her head drooped forward. From the folds of His robe, He took a simple gold crown and placed it gently upon her humbly bowed head. He offered her a piece of bread to eat and spoke tenderly.

"Farah, I love you. You belong to Me."

The voice was kind, yet behind it she sensed a power like water cascading over great falls. Farah felt a transformation deep in her soul. She was new, forever changed by the purifying fire of His presence.

When Farah awoke from her dream, the smile she had fallen asleep with had grown into a grin that enveloped her entire face.

The feelings and the encounter . . . with Jesus . . . lingered. *Yes,* she thought, *it was a dream, but it was also* real.

The Man she had met was the King, and now she felt every bit His daughter. For the first time in her life, she knew she was worth something. Even the self-confidence she'd had in her days of freedom and success with Rania was nothing compared to this. Now she knew; now she *mattered.*

EARTHLY ENCOUNTER

Jamal eyed Farah suspiciously. She hummed cheerfully while serving dinner, and as always, she served Jamal first, then the boys, and lastly, herself.

Jamal sampled his food and stared at Farah savoring hers as if it were the only meal she'd ever eaten. The woman seemed not to notice his look. She was far away in thought and spirit, remembering her meeting the night before.

Jamal didn't like her focus being anywhere other than on him. Today, though, he found his wife's manner disturbing but fascinating. He studied her face and her body language, then began asking questions about her day. Following the interrogation, Farah jumped up and, with a spring in her step, gathered dirty dishes and hustled them into the kitchen. Jamal followed her, planning a showdown that would include a beating.

He raised his hand to strike her from behind, but Farah anticipated the move. She whirled, looked her threatening husband in the eye, and with the most conviction she'd ever felt, shouted at him.

"No! You will not hit me, Jamal! You cannot do this to me

anymore. I'm no longer a Muslim. I'm a child of the King! Do you understand me?"

Stunned by the incomprehensible rebuke, Jamal froze. After staring at Farah in disbelief for several seconds, he dropped the raised hand to his side.

Jamal Samaha merely turned and walked away.

IN PERSON WITH JOANN

I met Farah one-on-one and talked with her over a cup of hot tea. She shared with me about her ongoing relationship with Jamal and how Jesus was helping her, but she also offered a challenge to all of us.

> **JoAnn:** People reading your story are no doubt teetering on the edges of their seats wondering about Jamal. He's seen the dramatic changes in you, but has he come to believe in Jesus as Savior?

> **Farah:** I wish I could say he has. However, I see that Jamal is on a journey and has been for a little over a year now. His eyes follow me as I go about my chores, as I care for the children, even in my rare moments of quiet solitude. He thinks I don't notice the questioning or longing I see flicker across his face, but I do.

> The beatings have stopped—which is a miracle in itself. You must understand, this is uncommon in my culture. Many of my new sisters in Jesus have

husbands who are Muslim. Their husbands continue to beat, berate, and abuse them. I clearly recognize I've been given a rare gift—and responsibility.

Paul taught that our lives are letters nonbelievers read, inscribed not with pen and ink but with the Spirit of the Living God. When Jamal is watching me, I know he is reading the letter the Holy Spirit is writing on my heart. He is seeing Jesus in me. He may not understand; in fact, I know he doesn't. But I see a longing mingled with confusion. It's just a matter of time before Jamal believes.

All of us—my believing friends and me—are praying for Jamal and our families to come to know Jesus as we do. I'm not ashamed of the gospel of Christ! I share Jesus with Jamal and my family—actually, with anyone who will listen—at every opportunity. Jesus is the most important One in my life!

JoAnn: Farah, your story illuminates the intimate love and mercy of Jesus when circumstances are utterly out of our control, and I thank you for inviting us to share your journey. *Habibti,** tell us about the extraordinary day you call "the great cleansing."

Farah: It was one of my most cherished days ever. I had been a follower of Jesus for a short time, but my commitment to Jesus was as solid as cement, my love for Him as deep as the ocean, and my hunger for the Word of God was as endless as a newborn baby's. During Bible study one day, Rima—the woman who is discipling me—and I were reading from Acts 8 where Philip met a man from Ethiopia who was reading the book of Isaiah. The man didn't understand the scripture, but Philip, filled with the Holy Spirit, began with the very passage the man was reading and told him the good news about Jesus. When they saw some water, the man asked Philip, "What prevents me from being baptized?" [v. 36 ESV]. And he was!

Well, the Holy Spirit tugged on my heart. After all, the Ethiopian was baptized immediately after he believed, and I was already months old in Jesus. Rima saw my tears, handed me a tissue, and slipped me a piece of paper with details of an upcoming baptism service for new followers of Jesus. The Acts 8 Bible study was intentional and effective. I signed right up, though I would keep the secret from my family.

The day of baptism dawned full of hope and anticipation. I arrived early, my hair tucked into a black hijab, excitement bubbling in my heart. My fingers crinkled a piece of paper hidden in my pocket. On it was the verse I'd prepared in the wee hours of the morning to share.

One by one, new MBBs gathered, the buzz in the room growing with each beaming face. When everyone had arrived, the people in charge locked the doors and windows to ensure our safety.

We began with worship, and the singing quieted our hearts. Then Pastor Ahmad spoke from Romans 10:9–10, reminding us that faith in Jesus alone grants salvation: "If you confess with your mouth that Jesus is Lord and believe in your heart that God raised him from the dead, you will be saved" [v. 9 ESV]. He made it clear to each of us that baptism was our outward expression of an inward commitment to our Savior.

Then we sang again. I've never heard such a beautiful chorus as we raised our voices in harmony: "Holy, Holy, Holy! Lord God Almighty . . ."

Soon it was my turn. I can still feel the coolness of the water caressing my skin as I walked down the steps of the baptismal.

Pastor Ahmad asked me, "Farah, have you repented of your sins and trusted Jesus as your Lord and Savior, and have you forsaken all false religions?"

Pastor Ahmad's kind question startled me out of my personal reverie.

"Yes, I have."

"Farah, do you believe that Jesus is the Son of God, that He was born of a virgin, lived a perfect life, died on the cross for your sins, and was raised from the dead? Do you believe He sent His Spirit to dwell within you while He Himself lives to make intercession for you at the right hand of the Father?"

"Yes, I do."

"Do you have a verse of Scripture the Spirit of God has been speaking to you?"

"Yes! This is what Jesus has done for me," I said as I pulled out my paper. Then I read:

> He put a new song in my mouth,
>   a song of praise to our God.
> Many will see and fear,
>   and put their trust in the LORD. (Ps. 40:3 ESV)

"Then it is my honor to baptize you, my sister in Christ, in the name of the Father, the Son, and the Holy Spirit."

I felt as if time slowed down. With my fingers, I pinched my nose closed. The pastor's hand was over mine. My eyes squeezed shut as my knees bent.

It was like a bath with clothes on, yet this was special water. Tingling warmth spread through my body, starting with my arms and legs, then centering in my heart, my spirit. The Father was cleansing me within, cleaning the dirty vessel I was and changing me into something fresh and new. As I sprang out of the water, I felt sparkly clean and shining on the inside.

I lingered in the dressing room, reluctantly removing what I thought of as a sacred garment. I dressed without drying off, treasuring the precious droplets of water clinging to my skin. I let the air dry my hair so the purified feeling would stay with me as long as possible.

God knows I had so much filth for Jesus to wash away—so much anger, hate, and unforgiveness souring my soul. I found myself saying over and over again, "Thank You, Jesus!"

That was also the last day I wore the hijab and abaya. I am a daughter of the King, and I will no longer dress as a Muslim because I belong to Jesus. I am not a Muslim on the inside, so I will not dress like a Muslim on the outside.

JoAnn: How did your husband and family respond to this bold decision?

Farah: At first my husband was shocked. He didn't beat me, although I sure was expecting it. I think he saw such a change in me that he actually liked it.

Our families have responded much like Jamal. The biggest problem I've had is from our radical neighbors. They often throw rocks at me or spit on me because I don't wear a hijab. Once, a rock cut open Medo's cheek. Even Jamal wants to move to another, less radical neighborhood.

I believe this is further evidence that God is moving in Jamal's heart. What Satan means for evil, God will use for good.

JoAnn: Do you have any other thoughts you'd like to share?

Farah: My mother did survive the surgery, and in the end God used my forced marriage to bring me to Jesus. It was the most painful time in my life, but my wonderful Savior worked in the midst of my misery. People often ask what the biggest difference is in my life now that I have Jesus. The answer is peace. I still have problems with my husband. Things are better, but problems still exist. Now, though, peace and comfort are my companions. I feel like I live in heaven, not on earth. Before, it was hell—*worse* than earth. Amazing! Even before I get to the real heaven, it already feels like heaven here—all because of Jesus. I will never leave Him or forsake Him.

JoAnn: You have new friends reading this story and praying for you. What would you like to say to them?

Farah: I've been waiting for this question, JoAnn. I want my dear brothers and sisters in Christ to know how much I love them and thank them for praying for me. And I have a message for them.

I had an empty heart and wish someone had told me about Jesus years ago. That's why I tell everyone about Him now. My life is in danger, but I don't care. I only want to follow my Savior and be faithful. That is my goal in life.

I hope it is *your* goal as well. There are probably Muslims living near you. They need you, dear friend. If you do not become their friend and then share Jesus with them . . . who will?

Be sure of this: Islam is imploding. Muslims have never been more open to Jesus.

I beg of you . . . go out of your way. Visit the mosque near you. Go to Mediterranean restaurants. Do something to show the love of Jesus to Muslims.

As for me, I expect to die for Jesus. In the West, you probably won't have to die for Jesus. But . . . will you *live* for Him?

Habibti is an Arabic term of affection between women.

I will instruct you and teach you in the way you
    should go;
        I will counsel you with my eye upon you.
        —PSALM 32:8 ESV

CHAPTER 4

THE LIAR FROM LEBANON

"Jihad al-nikah."

Layla Medina sifted the repugnant words through clenched teeth. She stared at the stream of black-robed figures moving past the window of her apartment.

Dark eyes from Tunisia and other parts of Syria—most belonging to teenage girls, a few women in their twenties, none older than thirtysomething—peered through the openings in each niqab. "Sexual jihad" was now official.

A few years before, Lotfi Ben Jeddou, interior minister of Tunisia, had told the Constituent Assembly of Tunisia that girls were traveling from his country to Syria, offering themselves in temporary marriage to Islamic State fighters. He honored their contribution, *giving comfort* to Muslim warriors during the continuing war against Bashar al-Assad.

Layla seethed as she recalled a report in which some of these "devoted" women bragged of servicing anywhere from fifty to one hundred different men. She adjusted her own niqab, took the hand of her six-year-old son, Bishara, and headed out her front door. On her way to the souk to buy lentils and bread for her family's evening meal, she joined the migration of women doing their part in the holy war.

Some managed to walk casually, but Layla could sense the revolting pride among the jihad al-nikah warriors. Even though only their eyes were visible, they obviously wanted everyone to acknowledge their *act of service* for the ISIS cause. Dozens moved every day along the streets that ran just north of the Euphrates River near downtown Raqqa, Syria. It was the path to government buildings seized from Assad's troops by the terrorists.

Islamic State leaders validated the twisted practice. They encouraged the volunteer sex slaves by bragging about the number of women who had joined the great fight against Bashar al-Assad and the Alawite-led government of Syria.

As Layla drifted among the other females, she conversed with herself about the spectacle and sneered, unseen behind her covering, at the women she passed. She tightened her grip on Bishara's hand and whispered under her breath, "These women fool themselves into thinking they're serving Allah. But they're serving only the lusts of men. They strut around Raqqa like princesses, their arrogance as offensive as the stench of their rancid perfume.

"And how does the great Islamic State have any time to fight the Syrian Arab Army? They're too busy with women."

She paused as a new thought entered her stream of conversation. "And how is it okay for men to have as many wives as they want? For a woman to do that would mean a death sentence." She squinted at a group of women. "Except in war, of course. Then we can have as *many* men as we want!

"These streetwalkers make me want to vomit. I don't care if they do want to help bring down Assad. Anytime women throw themselves at men—in war or peace—they are *whores*."

Layla stopped and eyed a group of about thirty women gathered in front of a partially bombed-out building. Several danced happily. Layla's insides boiled as a woman wearing a hijab emerged from the building and pointed in turn to each of five dark forms and motioned them to come with her. The giggles emitting from the niqabs told Layla that the chosen ones were teenagers. She watched the deluded girls disappear inside the dismal structure.

Layla wagged her head in disgust, resumed her slow walk toward the marketplace, and continued the conversation with herself.

"So much for the Islamic State and its fine security. The SAA doesn't need intelligence reports or GPS to find our troops. All they have to do is look for the lines of women waiting to do their part. Then they can just drop bombs there."

Despite their gleeful movements and giggles, Layla imagined shame in the girls' eyes.

"How deceived these women are. Can they really believe they'll gain husbands for doing their part to win the war? Who would want them after this? They will have destroyed their lives and won't have a chance for another *husband* until the next war in Syria." She chuckled derisively. "Of course, the way things are going, that won't be very long."

Layla walked a block in silence and then began a new tirade inside her niqab. "Is this what my religion teaches about women? Are we good only for sex and babies? Our Qur'an would beg to differ, I suppose. Even though I've never read it, I intend to now. I'm tired of hearing the imams tell me what the Qur'an says. I'll read it myself, and then I'll straighten them out.

"Yes, and this perversion of the role of women in Islam will cease! I will go to Muhammad and read *his* words. He loved us dearly."

Layla stopped short, realizing that the volume of her muttering had increased, and Bishara was watching her. Worse, Layla could not avoid the next thought, something she had heard countless times since she was a young girl: *The Great Prophet enjoyed thirteen wives during his life.* Every imam she'd ever known had reminded her of that monumental fact.

A WOMAN'S PLACE, A WOMAN'S DISGRACE

The scent of coffee dregs mingled with stale cigarette smoke in the unpleasant way that reminded Layla she was at home. She sat on the couch and stared pensively at an emerald book on the coffee table. Yasser had left it, as always, beside a chipped cup half full of cold coffee and an ashtray overflowing with cigarette butts.

Hands trembling, Layla reached for the book. She was about to read the Qur'an for herself for the first time. The anticipation was both exhilarating and frightening.

Layla fingered the pages. Their softness soothed her tense body.

Although she had never held the book, she noticed the gold had worn off the page edges from Yasser's daily ritual of reading. She held her breath momentarily at the thought that frightened her most: *Will I find the answers here that I'm looking for?*

Heart pounding, Layla leafed through the Islamic holy book. Not knowing exactly what she was looking for, she skimmed random pages until the following words caught her eye:

Men are in charge of women, because Allah hath made the one of them to excel the other, and because they spend of their property (for the support of women). So good women are the obedient, guarding in secret that which Allah hath guarded. As for those from whom ye fear rebellion, admonish them and banish them to beds apart, and scourge them. (Qur'an 4:34)[1]

Layla caught her breath. Tears began to form in the corners of her eyes. She heaved, then broke into inconsolable sobs.

Unwanted but undeniable thoughts raced through her mind. *This is one of the ugly truths our so-called holy book teaches about women. Yes, I know firsthand how women are treated. The scars on my body are proof. I've survived my whole life under the black cloud of cruelty that Islam claims is part of a "peaceful religion," but I never knew the surahs actually said such awful and degrading things. How could our religion teach such hate? How can I continue to believe and revere my faith?*

"Oh, God," she finally said aloud, "but this is all I've ever known and what I've been taught and believed since I was a girl!"

For three months Layla pored over the Qur'an, determined to understand how she could have misunderstood her first reading.

She took notes on every passage that mentioned women. She pondered her readings for hours. She wondered. And she cried.

She also hid her study from Yasser. He would never approve of her reading the Qur'an. Since the day they were married, he had reminded her that he would read it *for her*, so she could "properly understand it." The day after their wedding ten years ago, he had insisted that she sit down and write out his instructions to her.

This is the most important book in the world, Layla. Nothing can match its wisdom. It is marvelous indeed. But women do not have the intellectual capability to grasp it. That is why I will read parts of it to you. Through me, you will come to understand it. That is why Allah has granted women to be married to men like me.

We are superior in our capacity to fathom the great things of our God. I will be your teacher. And it is important for me to make sure that you learn the Qur'an. So I will test you on it each week. If you are not able to answer my questions, it is only fair for you to be punished. Allah wills it, of course!

But I am a gifted teacher. Our esteemed imam in Raqqa often tells me this. So I have no doubt that you will be my A-plus student. My only student.

And I cannot wait for you to teach our children. They will be mighty for Allah. If we don't overthrow the illegitimate Assad terrorist regime, their generation most certainly will. Yes, they will continue in our footsteps, take up our work, and finish what we started. Syria will one day be in the rightful control of Sunni Muslims again, and the Alawites will be banished from the home of Allah's true Arab warriors, the Islamic State.

Layla, come sit at my feet and learn the way of
Muhammad. You will not want me to stop teaching you. I
know this to be true. Sharia law is the future of the world,
and no one knows it better than me.

One afternoon while studying alone at the house, Layla
reread Yasser's instructions and burst into laughter.

She spoke to the empty room: "Oh Yasser, if you are such
a gifted teacher, why do I have more doubts about my religion
than when I married you? I'm sure that's a question you will not
be able to answer."

After ninety days of searching the Qur'an, one central question had formed in Layla's mind: Were the inconsistencies she
saw in her religion from the Qur'an or from her husband's life?

After a month of reading Hadith, Islam's second holiest book,
Layla had amassed only more questions. She realized, too, that
her husband's vicious behavior could be directly related to what
he learned from the Qur'an and Hadith.

Overwhelming questions bombarded her thoughts day and
night:

- *How can I stay a Muslim? Especially in light of the abysmal
  treatment of women. We are despised!*
- *Even the prophet Muhammad's wife Aisha said her arms were
  green with bruises. And she was one of the lucky ones! She was a
  loved woman. Islam has elevated the abuse of women and made
  it standard behavior in our world. Why has such evil become
  mainstream in our society?*

• *I will never have the life I dreamed of with my husband. I will always be less than him. Should I just take little Bishara and disappear?*

FREE FROM SYRIA, CAPTIVE IN LEBANON

Although Layla's questions remained unanswered, plans for her future took on a life of their own one morning just after Yasser left for work. Within minutes he had returned. Bursting into the living room, he barked at his wife.

"Layla, get clothes for you and Bishara. The Syrian Arab Army is going to throw me in prison or kill me. We must go now! They know where we live."

Layla cowered momentarily, afraid that her husband's powerful voice would tip off the neighbors to their plan. Then she looked at her husband, puzzled.

"Yasser, what did you do to be singled out like this? You're a car salesman, not a terrorist. Why would they care about you?"

"It doesn't matter, Layla. I'll tell you on the way to Beirut. I do more than sell cars. I help the cause too." He tapped his chest. "I'm a vehicle supplier for the Islamic State. Go wake Bishara. We have to go!"

Minutes later Yasser had procured a taxi, and the Medina family was heading west toward the Lebanon border. Layla had despised Syrian refugees throughout the war. In her eyes they were weak traitors.

As if reading Layla's thoughts, Yasser assured her that they would never become refugees. This trip would be merely a temporary leave from Syria until the heat was off. The SAA would soon be defeated, and if they weren't, they would forget about Yasser and assume he was out of Syria for good.

Layla had her doubts.

"But, Yasser, how are we going to get through the border to Lebanon? It's not like Syria is letting people into Lebanon from Raqqa. They know it's the capital of the Islamic State. They won't let us through."

"I have friends at the border, Layla." He smirked. "It also helps that I'm having a car delivered to the Syrian commander at the Qaa border crossing." He shot a glance at Layla. "Don't think of it as a bribe. Think of it as a present for his family that will facilitate our crossing. He'll alert the commander on the Lebanon side." He winked. "I have a gift for him too. Not a car. But it's what every soldier needs: money."

As the taxi sped toward the Syrian coast, Layla realized that Yasser's meticulous plan had been in place for a while. She pointed at the driver.

"Yasser, you never told him where we are going, but he already knew where to take us, didn't he?"

Yasser grinned, his satisfaction obvious as he nodded smugly.

"I've had our escape plan in place for the last three years. That's how I know this trip to Lebanon will be for just a short time. We will be back to Syria soon enough. And when we return, it will be a new country with the Islamic State in power. Syria will be the headquarters of the Arab world, and the Islamic State and our Sharia law will spread out from *our* home city. Muslims everywhere will see us as the model of how we will one day rule the whole world!"

His devilish laugh woke Bishara from a nap, frightened and crying as if he'd been having a bad dream. Layla stroked her son's head and admitted to herself that she felt the same dread.

NEW LIFE, NEW LAND, NEW LOW

"Consider it a token of appreciation, *habibi!*[2] Really, Hisham. It's nothing at all." Yasser schmoozed the border commander.

Along the seven-hour drive from Raqqa, the Medinas had endured grueling checkpoints, but now they were getting VIP treatment where it mattered most—from Yasser's new friend Hisham and the rest of the military staff at the border.

With a two-year-old Toyota Corolla from Yasser's dealership as their admission ticket, the Medina family skated through the Syrian crossing. Complementary coffee and fresh baklava added to the delight of passing the border, and as their car accelerated into Lebanon, Yasser pointed over his shoulder.

"Layla, look at that sign. It will surely be gone the next time we see this border."

Layla turned to read the banner over the Lebanese checkpoint: "Welcome to Bashar al-Assad's Syria. The Lebanese and the Syrians are one people that live in two brotherly lands."

Yasser sneered as he continued. "I tell you this: the sickening face of Assad will be down, and the symbol of the Islamic State will be in place of that criminal. We will one day see his body swinging in the wind when he is captured by our rebel heroes. His end is coming soon." He raised his hand. "Goodbye for now, my sweet land of Syria."

Two months later Yasser's brilliant escape plan appeared to be anything but brilliant. The friends who had invited the Medinas to stay with them had a change of heart once their own relatives arrived as refugees. As a result, Yasser, Layla, and Bishara had no place to stay, and the money that seemed endless was dwindling.

Worse, a surge in the war closed the borders and guaranteed that no one who had come from Raqqa would be let back into Syria. With the Islamic State on the run, it would be suicidal for partisans like Yasser to go back now. The only welcome he would receive would be a prison sentence or a bullet through his head. Angry but resigned to his fate, Yasser headed to the camp near Tripoli, Lebanon's northern city, where he registered his family as Syrian refugees.

Syrian refugees. The gravity of the label settled upon Layla as camp authorities assigned Yasser, Bishara, and Layla each a number and then directed them to a tent.

Layla peeled open the tarp and stared through tears at the filthy, minuscule space that had become their new home. She noted that one small heater offered the only hope of warmth during cold weather; then she smiled at Bishara while everything inside her collapsed. Her life was over, and she could tell Yasser felt that he had just made the biggest mistake of his life. Surely there would've been a safe place to go somewhere in Syria.

Their days in Beddawi camp stretched into weeks, and after six months, Yasser slipped into a crushing depression. Layla's once verbose Muslim teacher rarely spoke, and he no longer read the Qur'an.

Layla feared her husband's despair even more than she had feared his domination, and she realized that if anything good was to come out of their mess, she would have to find it. *I'm in charge now.* She blinked every time the thought passed through her mind.

Yasser had been a wheeler-dealer in Syria, but now he was just a number—part of the Syrian refugee disaster. The Lebanese people had long ago come to disdain the burden of caring for thousands who escaped the madness in Syria. It didn't matter whether the numbered refugees had arrived legally or illegally. Most Lebanese people just wanted them gone.

Syrians used to look down their noses at their Lebanese neighbors, whom they considered weak and easily controlled by outsiders. But now the tables were turned. This was payback time.

Yasser did little each day other than sleep and drink. Loneliness eroded Layla's spirit, and she gave up her personal study of the Qur'an about women in Islam. She had no time for questions now. Survival was all that mattered.

Fights occurred daily in Beddawi as old scores were settled between enemies now thrown too closely together. Although the food was tolerable, boredom smothered Layla even as she played with Bishara. She hoped her son would think everything would be fine. Yet after brief respites, Layla's fear of being in charge always returned. Life with Yasser had never been up to her before, and she had no idea what to do next.

But that was about to change.

A SHOULDER TO CRY ON

"Welcome to Lebanon! I see you're new here."

Layla had been standing in front of her tent, gazing at nothing in particular when the loud but sweet voice startled her.

"How are you adjusting to the camp? I'm sure it's been hard for you. I know it was for me. But moving here from Syria actually has turned out to be the best thing that ever happened to my whole family."

The chatty woman paused. "Oh, silly me! Here I am rambling on, and I haven't even introduced myself. I'm from Aleppo, and my name is Dina Hadad."

Layla's eyes focused on the woman.

"Dina, it's nice to meet you." Her desperation disallowed any pretense of doing well. "Can we go somewhere and talk?"

Without waiting for an answer, Layla grabbed Bishara's hand and pulled him up from his seat by the wall of their tent. Dina nodded and motioned for the two to follow her.

Once they were inside the coffee tent, Layla's composure shattered. Unable to speak, she sobbed, out of control. Seeing Bishara's distress at his mother's condition, Dina reached for the boy and pulled him slowly into her arms. An hour later Layla was still weeping.

Through deep breaths Layla began to choke out her story to the kind stranger. "Not only do we have no idea when we will get out of this godforsaken place, but Palestinians have been here for decades—and they hate us too. This camp is falling apart! Did you know that it's been here since 1955? Can you believe it, Dina? We're overrun with rats. And to think Yasser and I had money in Syria, and we left it all behind."

She stopped abruptly, panting. "I'm sorry, Dina. I haven't even heard your story. How did *you* end up here?"

Dina smiled at the question. "Every day, Layla, I ask God who He wants me to meet, and today it was you. I wasn't sure why I was drawn to your tent. This is my first visit to Beddawi camp. But I've learned to trust the Spirit to lead me. This is my story: my friends tell me that I had the worst marriage in Syria." She laughed charmingly. "Now that's a great honor, isn't it?

"I think my friends were right, though. Because of the beatings and all the other women my husband had, I dreamed of not just leaving my husband; I wanted to *kill* him! But then a miracle happened: Mohammad was saved."

Dina's statement hung in the air, and Layla wondered what in the world it meant that he "was saved."

"Your husband was *saved*? Saved from what?"

Dina giggled. "Mohammad was saved from his *sins*. That's the most important thing to be saved from. God may save us from danger and harm, but that's only temporary. And let me tell you, that man had a lot of sins to be saved from. But Jesus forgave him, and *I* had to forgive him."

Tears drying on her face, Layla cocked her head and looked at Dina, puzzled. Slowly, comprehension replaced the confusion.

"Dina, what are you doing talking about Jesus? You're a Muslim!"

Dina scanned the other tables nearby, paused for a second in thought, and said, "Let's go for a walk, Layla. We need some privacy."

During several laps around the refugee camp, Dina told the daring account of her conversion. Her heart laid bare, she drew Layla into her world of redemption. The two women crafted a plan, and by the end of the conversation, Layla had the answer to what she would do next.

MEETING THEM, MEETING HIM

Layla Medina could not believe she was actually going to a church, but she had to find out why Dina felt such freedom and joy, like Layla had always wanted. How could Jesus have anything to do with that? After all, wasn't He just a prophet?

As Layla and Bishara stepped off the midmorning bus arriving in Tripoli, Dina and her husband, Mohammad, waved excitedly. When they were close enough to be heard over the street noise, Dina pointed at Mohammad and hollered.

"Marhaba, Layla! This is my husband, Mohammad. He's the one I wanted to kill." Dina laughed as she blurted out the cold facts.

Mohammad laughed at the awkward introduction, too, and smiled sweetly at his wife.

"Hi, Layla, I'm Mohammad, and let me tell you, my wife had the right to kill me for everything I put her through. But Jesus delivered both of us, and we've . . . well, we've never been more in love. After Dina told me about you and your situation, I've been praying for you, and I believe God has heard your cry. Jesus is coming to your rescue."

Layla marveled at how freely the Hadads shared about—and laughed about—the pain they'd been through.

"Marhaba to both of you! I must say, I've never heard an introduction like that."

Dina shook her head, marveling at her own new life, and said loud enough for other passengers getting off the bus to hear: "Sorry about that, Layla. We're just amazed at how powerful our Jesus is! Let's get some breakfast, and then we'll head for the church. Okay?"

Layla put her index finger over her mouth to shush the Hadads. "I think you should be more careful talking about Jesus so openly in public. You both come from well-known Muslim families in Syria and Lebanon. You could get killed."

Dina took a deep breath as a smile spread across her face.

"You're right, Layla. We probably should be more careful. Our families have put a fatwa on our lives. So has an imam in Aleppo. But when we gave our lives to Jesus, we resigned ourselves to the fact that we would probably die for Him. He is *so* worth it, Layla!" She tugged her friend's arm. "Let's go!"

Layla's shock over the Hadads' openness was surpassed by her reaction to the smiling refugees at the Tripoli Baptist Church. She recognized several of them from Beddawi. But how could they be happy?

A man approached while Layla was lost in thought.

"Layla, I've heard all about you! My name is Rafik, and I'm so glad you've come. My wife and I organize the food and clothing drive here at the church. I hope you don't mind, but Dina told us some of your story. I'm sorry things have been so tough for you. I think they're about to get better, though."

"What makes you so sure about that, Rafik?" Layla said with a smirk, a hand placed coyly on her hip.

"I've also heard that you say what's on your mind without holding back. That's important, you know. When the disciple Nathanael met Jesus for the first time, his friends had told him Jesus was from Nazareth. And at that, Nathanael asked, 'Can anything good come out of Nazareth?' [John 1:46 ESV]. Nazareth was kind of the joke of the day, and I think Jesus actually enjoyed the jab."

Rafik paused, then swept his hand toward the building.

"We have food here for lunch, and you can take your pick of anything you need in the piles of clothes. Also, please help yourself to the food boxes. And while you're getting acquainted around the place, can I hold little Bishara?"

Layla looked puzzled. "How did you know his name is Bishara?"

Rafik leaned toward Layla. "My wife, Miriam, and I have been praying for you and your whole family since Dina told us about you yesterday." He turned to the boy. "Let's go, Bishara! Do you like soccer?"

As Rafik left with Bishara, Dina took Layla by the arm and walked her into the church.

"I know this is all new for you—I mean meeting people with Muslim names who now follow Jesus. Don't worry about it, though. It's happening all over the Muslim world. Did you know that, Layla?"

Layla shook her head and rolled her eyes. "No, I didn't know that, and it sounds positively insane to me, Dina. Why would people risk their lives like that? It doesn't make a lot of sense to me."

"I found the Truth, Layla. Once that happened, I knew I'd never be the same. The biggest issue for me was how our religion viewed women. I was sad when I read what the Qur'an says about us. But when I finally had the nerve to read the Bible, I saw how Jesus *valued* women. The difference was night and day. My husband, Mohammad, is living proof of that. Have you ever thought about the plight of women in Islam?"

Layla stiffened. "I don't even know what you're talking about, Dina. We have full rights in Islam, and our religion is the best thing that ever happened to women."

Frustrated at herself for lying about her real opinion, Layla feigned confidence and walked away toward the worship center. Dina watched Layla go and simply prayed for her.

Layla heard singing and approached the sanctuary eagerly. Suddenly she was up for a fight. Christianity was just another false religion, and she couldn't wait to tell others that it was. A Christian worship service would be the perfect place to load up on ammunition to report the truth about this pathetic faith. What she found inside, though, was hardly pathetic.

The singing, reading of the Bible, the teaching—all so foreign to Layla—warmed her frozen heart. She had never heard words of hope sprinkled so lavishly with love. Layla had been taught the Bible was dangerous, to stay away from it at all costs. She had heard that it had been rewritten, that it had been changed and was packed full of lies. Yet everything Layla heard that beautiful day in Tripoli was pleasant to her ears. She felt as if a glass of fresh water was pouring straight onto her parched soul.

When the worship service ended, Layla sat on the polished wood pew and stared blankly for several minutes at the red curtain behind the musicians who were putting away their instruments. She slowly realized that more than an hour and a half had elapsed since she had entered the sanctuary. Layla had sat on the edge of her seat in wonder the entire time. By contrast, at the mosque, she was usually so bored she could hardly keep her eyes open.

The music, the teaching—the spirit of this place—had pierced Layla at the core of her being. The secret place—she supposed it was her *soul*—that had never been penetrated before was laid bare by the Word of God.

Still, she couldn't quite decide if she was lighthearted because of the worship service, because of the warm people at this church, or simply because she had gotten away from the crabby inhabitants of the camp for a few blessed hours. She shook her head. No, this couldn't be real.

Her recovery complete, Layla stood as Rafik and Miriam walked up to the end of the pew where she had been sitting. Before they could ask how she liked the service, Layla offered her assessment.

"I didn't get anything out of that service! Strange songs for sure. Was the man speaking about the Bible? He lost me, and it just didn't make sense. Do you want to come to the mosque with me sometime? It's a slice of heaven on earth."

Lies again! Layla's inner conversation began immediately. *How could I say those things when I saw so much love in that room? My heart was full when that man spoke from the Bible.*

Despite the distant front she put on, Layla didn't want to leave the church. But it was five o'clock. She and Bishara needed to catch the bus back to Beddawi.

A QUESTION AT THE BREAKING POINT

Arriving back at her tent, Layla wished she hadn't returned. She found Yasser pacing the small interior, talking to himself and intermittently raging at their situation.

She slipped into the tent and set Bishara down to play on the dirt floor. As she rose up, her face collided with Yasser's fist.

"You better not have gone to that church, Layla. Someone told me you left with some refugees who go to a Baptist church in Tripoli. A Baptist church? This is *haram!*"[3]

She straightened herself from the blow and looked the hostile man in the eye.

"My dear Yasser, why is it that I went to a church and ended up meeting more friends and more people that care for me than I've *ever* met at a mosque? Ever!"

Yasser's answer was another fist to her face. This time Layla sprawled on the dirt floor, unconscious.

When she came to, she was alone in the tent. That Yasser had left didn't bother her in the least, but that he had evidently taken Bishara with him frightened her. She opened the tent flap and headed toward the sound of an imam screaming into a bullhorn. He was calling for the Islamic State to rise up in the camp.

Layla surveyed the burgeoning crowd for a full minute. When her eyes focused, she felt as if someone had kicked her in the stomach. Yasser was in the first row, Bishara in his lap with a fist raised in the air. *Like Daddy, like son.* At the thought, Layla felt nauseous.

Yasser had resumed his fundamentalist obsessions. Even though he hadn't practiced Islam in the slightest since arriving in Lebanon, Layla's church attendance triggered a renewed fanaticism. The old Yasser was back, and Layla knew her life was in danger.

She headed back to the tent and dropped into bed. How could the first part of the day have been filled with such joy and the second part so filled with terror? Fresh tears ran down her cheeks as she drifted off to sleep.

Layla! I see you. I know you're afraid. But I am with you.

In the middle of the night, the encounter happened.

"Who are you?"

Layla felt calm even though the mysterious but magnificent

Stranger in the dream didn't tell her His name. But His smile was unmistakable.

Layla, you know who I am. You know Me. And remember this: "A friend loves at all times" [Prov. 17:17].

The next morning Layla left with Bishara before Yasser even moved. She wanted answers about her dream even if it meant Yasser might beat her again for leaving.

"Bishara, my sweet one, you and Mommy are going on the bus again today. We're going to see our new friends."

The boy brightened at her words and began to skip toward the bus stop. Layla chuckled and began skipping with him.

At the church Rafik welcomed the two refugees with a question that shocked Layla.

"Hi, Layla and Bishara! I hope you had a good night and are doing well today." He paused briefly and smiled. "Hey, my wife had a women's Bible study last night at our house, and I was thinking about you. I wondered something: Layla, are you satisfied with your role as a woman in Islam?"

"Layla, are you satisfied with your role as a woman in Islam?" The words reverberated in her mind. Layla Medina managed not to signal her true reaction to the stunning question and faked her answer convincingly.

"Well, of course I am. Our religion honors women. We are esteemed and valued."

Layla summoned a confident smile for Rafik, then turned and walked away. But unstoppable thoughts flooded her mind. *Did Rafik see the fist mark on my face from last night? What the Qur'an says about women is horrible and demeaning! If I were in court, I'd be convicted of perjury. My heart screams, "No! How could a woman possibly be satisfied with Islam? We're treated worse than animals!" But I lied: "Of course, Rafik. I am satisfied." What a fake I am. I'm as bad as Yasser.*

The confrontation with Rafik—and with her own conscience—was too much for her. She and Bishara didn't even sit down. No one saw Layla sneak out the back door of the church. Nor did they see the tears streaming down her face.

An hour later she stepped off the bus with Bishara and headed straight for her tent. She picked up the holiest book of Islam. Layla would give the Qur'an one more try.

BACK TO THE TRUTH

Layla stayed away from the church for several weeks. How could she ever show her face there again? She had lied her way out of Rafik's overwhelming question, and she was sure he saw right through her.

She was right; he had recognized the lie. But even while Layla avoided the church, Rafik and Miriam made routine deliveries of food, clothes, and home goods for Layla and her family. Mohammad and Dina came often too. With Yasser's recommitment to hard-line Islam, though, explosions continued to erupt nightly in the Medina tent.

One evening Rafik, Miriam, Mohammad, and Dina stopped outside the tent, shocked by the screams emanating from inside. They were Layla's. Rafik called her name, and the scuffling inside stopped.

A hand threw back the tent flap, and the four visitors stepped toward the entrance. Layla spread several fingers across her face to hide a bruise and smiled weakly as she walked out. Sad eyes revealed her heartbreak, and the visitors wept inwardly for their friend.

Yasser's eyes narrowed, and he stared at the intruders for several seconds. They recognized the silent warning and pulled back. As the four walked away, each couple holding hands and praying out loud, Layla called out to them.

"Rafik! The answer to your question is *no*! I am not satisfied with my role as a woman. I never will be. Thank you for coming tonight."

Dina called back to her. "Layla, we are here for you! 'A friend loves at all times.'"

Layla froze at the words, then disappeared behind the blue tarp. The two couples stopped in their tracks, dropped to their knees, held hands, and prayed for Layla's protection that night.

The next morning Layla and Bishara were waiting outside the church before the morning crew arrived to greet refugees. Layla scanned the street, and after several minutes she saw what she was looking for. Rafik and Miriam rounded the corner and strolled casually toward the church. Layla grabbed Bishara's hand and sprinted toward them.

As soon as Miriam realized the woman running toward her was Layla, Miriam called out, "Are you okay?"

Panting, Layla stopped just before running over the couple. "Yes! Yes, I'm okay." Her face glowed. "Jesus rescued me last night."

Standing on the Tripoli sidewalk, Layla blurted out her story.

"I saw Him last night. I wasn't asleep. He came in a vision.

"After you four visited, Yasser was so angry about Christians coming around again, he threatened me like he never has before. I was afraid I was in for a long night, but as soon as Bishara was down for the night, Yasser suddenly left for an ISIS rally.

"I was sitting on the floor, thinking about how I've lied to you even though all you've done is try to help me. And you knew I was lying, yet you still loved me. I feel closer to you than my own family. Miriam, you and Dina care for me more than my own sisters. You *are* my sisters.

"For you to come to Beddawi camp as Christians was dangerous, but you came anyway. Even being in Tripoli is dangerous. When the welcome sign in the square reads The City of Islam, that's not a place for Christians—especially ones who talk openly about Jesus.

"When I was finally alone, I said, 'Jesus, I want truth. I'm tired of lies—the lies I tell and the lies that have been told to me by my religion. I want out of my life. I want to start over. Jesus, are you God?'"

Layla stared for several seconds past the couple and up the street, then continued. "All of a sudden there was a flash of light in the tent, and *He was there.*"

"Who was there?" Miriam asked just as Dina and Mohammad ambled up.

"It was *Jesus.* He told me this: 'My truth lives in your new friends. It will live in you soon. I am the way, the truth, and the life. No one comes to the Father except through Me. Layla, do you believe?'

"I bowed my face to the ground and said, 'Yes, Jesus. Yes!'

"Then He was gone. But the light remained. In fact, as I sat there, several neighbors came by and asked me, 'Where did you get your lights?'

"When Yasser returned, even he saw the heavenly glow on my face *and* the light. It made such an impression on him that he asked me, 'Are you okay, Layla?'

"I told Yasser, 'I've never been better in my life.' And I told the neighbors, 'You can't buy the light in our tent. It's not from this world.'

"Yasser was so stunned, he didn't say a mean word to me all night, and he didn't beat me. Even he seemed to sense we were on holy ground." Layla shook her head. "I have never in my whole life slept so peacefully."

She looked each of her listeners in the eye, then added, "I'm ready. You are my family; now lead me to Jesus, please. But first I must do this."

Layla unwrapped her hijab and took it off. When she looked up, tears flowed.

"Now I'm ready for Jesus."

Dina led in prayer, and all five friends cried through it. Layla lifted her head, radiating joy.

"Well, family, there's only one thing left to do." Layla smiled. "I'm going to tell Yasser."

IN PERSON WITH TOM AND JOANN

Over lunch in the ancient city of Byblos, Lebanon, Layla shared the rest of her story with JoAnn.

> **JoAnn:** Layla, your story of Jesus coming to you thrills my heart. What's happened since then?
>
> **Layla:** Dina and Miriam are discipling me. I'm learning so much! I just love the Word of God. I'm consumed by it and devour it each day. Little Bishara has given his life to Jesus too.

JoAnn: What about Yasser? How did he take the news?

Layla: I went straight to him and told him that day. I braced myself for violence, but it never came. He knew something was up when I walked through the camp without my hijab on.

He listened to me and my story. I even apologized to him for how much I hated him, and he was stunned. Only God could've softened Yasser's heart like that.

I've learned so much from Dina and have prayed for a miracle like she's seen in Mohammad's life. But it hasn't happened yet. The deep things of God that He does in a person's life often come after much prayer.

JoAnn: Do you share your faith with others?

Layla: Every day! Dina and I go to the refugee camps and tell other women our stories. They are thirsty for Jesus. We've had several near escapes from death. Yet this is what we expected. Jesus promised persecution, so we were ready for it.

JoAnn: Layla, do you have any final words for the friends reading your story?

Layla: Yes—I sure do. My life verse is this: "You will know the truth, and the truth will set you free" (John 8:32).

I want to say this to wives and mothers: Dina saw a miracle with Mohammad and then in her own life. I saw one in my life. I'm still waiting and watching for Jesus to open Yasser's eyes and heart. I know the miracle is coming.

Don't give up, women of God. If your husband needs Christ or one of your children does, keep praying.

Jesus showed me the truth. He *is* the Truth. Are you desperate enough for Jesus to move in your loved ones' lives that you're willing to pray, fast, and get on your face before God each day? I do this in my tent. Join me in fervent prayer for our families.

Jesus is moving mountains in my life. He will in yours too.

Jesus is also saving souls in Tripoli. People are fed up with war and all the killing. In fact, the city recently took down the City of Islam sign and replaced it with another sign that reads "The City of Peace."

Always remember this: Jesus is the Truth; He is the only One who can set you free. I am certainly proof of that.

And, dear family in the West, your sister Layla is praying for you from the Beddawi camp in Tripoli, Lebanon. I love you deeply in Christ.

The times of ignorance God overlooked, but now he commands all people everywhere to repent.
—Acts 17:30 esv

CHAPTER 5

HOPELESS—THEN JESUS ARRIVED

The dead bolt clicked loudly in a heavy metal door. Curtains slid shut. One by one, women in drab hijabs entered furtively from a side entrance.

They exchanged enthusiastic hugs and cheek kisses. Then, after a head count, padlocks snapped into place on the door they had entered. Lights dimmed, and the weekly women's Bible study meeting for former Muslims was ready to begin. In a fundamentalist city renowned for its honor killings, no security precaution was too extreme.

Roughly a dozen women settled into chairs. Nervous excitement rippled through the group at the presence of a special guest. Naima, the group leader, smiled and asked each participant to introduce herself to the American woman named JoAnn.

When my turn came for an introduction, I asked if they felt comfortable removing their hijabs. As the ladies gently unwrapped the coverings from around their faces, I tried not to let my jaw drop at the beauty disclosed before my eyes. Radiant smiles widened even further as the women were seen for who they are.

I asked if we could hear their stories because I knew each one had endured more than I could imagine, and I was right. The evening produced more firsthand accounts of Jesus' miracles than I've ever heard in any one meeting. Jamila spoke first while Naima translated for us.

Jamila Speaks About Defying the Death Sentence

My fate was clear. It was too late for any reprieve. I was set to die, and there was nothing I could do about it. Even if I could have moved, it was no use.

I would shortly depart this world from Deir ez-Zor, Syria, like so many others during our miserable war, but it wasn't the Islamic State that pronounced my death sentence. It was Dr. Basil Hussein, one of the most respected neurologists in Syria. He explained to my family the end that he believed was inevitable.

"I'm sorry to tell the Darwish family this news, but a blood vessel ruptured, and Jamila experienced a massive stroke. If only she could have had her blood pressure medicine." He spoke wistfully.

"I know medical supplies and prescriptions are scarce

and too expensive for most people, but this was preventable." His voice was sad. "But then, maybe these days, it is not preventable in Deir ez-Zor.

"Jamila is paralyzed on her right side, and I just don't see how she can come out of this coma. Her vitals are extremely erratic. My best guess is that she may have a day or two left—unless Allah intervenes, of course. I apologize for saying this to you, but it's time to plan her funeral."

What no one in my hospital room knew was that I had clearly heard every one of the doctor's words. My mother and sisters burst into tears at my bedside.

I couldn't talk, couldn't move. Alone in my mind, I cried at my hopeless, helpless situation. The isolation crushed me. But then, suddenly, I was not alone. The room erupted in dazzling light, and a Man stood at the foot of my bed.

He smiled and called my name. *Jamila, I am Jesus! I hear you've been looking for Me.*

In my most extreme dreams, I could not have imagined this, but Jesus stood in my room. Even though I was a practicing Muslim, I knew who He was. The Qur'an speaks of Jesus. And I'd also heard that He had been appearing miraculously to people during the Syrian war.

In fact, I remembered thinking one day previously when life was beyond hard that I wished Jesus would visit me. There was so much hate all around. But Jesus was about love—so I had heard. And we needed some of that in Syria.

Evidently He knew I had wished for His presence because He said to me, *Jamila, I know your longing for*

Me to visit you. I've heard your cries. Here I am. I've come to heal you for My glory.

I wondered if this was really happening or if it was a hallucination brought on by my medications, or maybe it was just a crazy dream. Then . . . Jesus touched my hand—my paralyzed hand—and heat instantly diffused through my whole body.

I heard my mother shout, "Dr. Hussein! Jamila's hand just moved! Did you see it?"

I could hear her jump out of the chair next to my bed.

Dr. Hussein stepped next to the bed and hovered above me with my family, looking for signs of movement. He was skeptical.

"I didn't see her move. Are you sure, Mrs. Darwish? I just don't think so."

I could hear nurses checking monitors. Dr. Hussein was telling family members that my vitals did not show anything indicating improvement when, suddenly, I felt like reaching out to Jesus. My right hand lifted in worship, and Jesus, still at the foot of my bed, smiled lovingly at me.

I heard screams in the room and a thud on the floor as my mother passed out cold.

Dr. Hussein yelled through the chaos, "Is she trying to grab someone's hand?"

I actually was! I desperately wanted to touch Jesus—like the woman with the issue of blood who touched the hem of His garment.

I know Jesus could have healed me instantaneously. He has the power to do that. But it's possible that my family might have thought I just snapped out of the coma, and Dr. Hussein had simply been wrong in his diagnosis.

So over the next few days, Jesus healed me progressively. Each time, He touched a different part of my body.

After my hand, it was my right leg. Jesus came in a vision the following morning, and with just one finger He touched my knee. The paralysis left instantly.

The next day I gained a full range of motion in my neck and shoulders. My face muscles began to work, except that my eyes would not open, and I still could not speak.

But then, another day later, my eyes and mouth opened while my whole family watched. I looked straight up, my eyes staring toward the ceiling, as Jesus faded from the room.

The first words I heard my father say were *"Allahu akbar! Allahu akbar!"** But my first words were "Jesus, Jesus, don't leave me! I love You."

That certainly quieted the room. My shocked family could not comprehend the words that hung in the air.

Then . . . *boom!* A massive explosion in the street interrupted the stunned silence.

In Deir ez-Zor, peace is short lived. Even after a great miracle like I experienced, the brutal reality of war set in. Oil fields—and the massive Conoco oil facility—along our part of the Euphrates River means that in eastern Syria no city is more coveted by international powers. Iran, Russia, and America are all there.

Our morbid history includes the slaughter of Armenians by the Turks in 1915 to show that Islam triumphed over

Christianity. And at the time of my healing, the Islamic State maintained a strong presence in the city to prove that they were the new champions of the Muslim faith. Chaos, carnage, and confusion were normal in Deir ez-Zor.

After Jesus healed me, the war worsened, and my family fled Syria. We could go either north to Turkey or south to Jordan, but the border in northern Syria was nearly impassable because of Turkey's battle against the Kurds. So we headed south.

The streets in Jerash, Jordan, didn't look much different than the streets of Deir ez-Zor. Refugees have nothing to do, so even many of the men had no work to go to during the day. But I was on a mission. I wanted to find Jesus—somehow.

Where could I go, I wondered, *to find out more about the Man who had healed me?* Obviously I couldn't talk openly to anyone with my family present. Although they often discussed the healing in my life, they gave credit to Allah, not to Jesus. Yet I knew the truth.

Then one day in the outdoor market, I saw a woman wearing a cross necklace. In Deir ez-Zor, you could get killed for doing that, but I guessed Jordan must be a little laxer.

I followed her, working up the courage to ask a question. When she stopped at a vegetable stand, I saw my chance as she was picking out cucumbers.

"Jesus healed me of paralysis when I was in a coma."

I blurted out the words and could see that I'd startled the woman. *Who is this mysterious person in a burka talking about Jesus?* she must have wondered.

"Do you know how I can find out more information about Jesus? I'm a Muslim, so I think I have a lot to learn. And marhaba. My name is Jamila. What's yours?"

The woman just looked at me for a moment, then introduced herself as Maria. And had Jesus ever led me to the right person!

Despite my abrupt, awkward self-introduction, Maria was warm and gracious. Over tea during the next couple of weeks, we became good friends. I asked her every question I could think of about Jesus. Although I was already convinced that Jesus had all power and was the Savior of the world, I had to know what it would be like to become a believer in a radical Muslim family.

When Maria told me that I was the one sent by God to reach my family, I was ready. I gave my life to Jesus; it was a day I will never forget!

The glorious thing is that Maria was right. Over time, every single person in my family—including my father—came to faith in Christ. What a miracle! It's rare that a family of people who practice fundamentalist Islam all become believers. So I am privileged and blessed beyond anything I could have imagined. Jesus used the miracle of my healing to open the hearts of my family.

Still, it wasn't easy. The process took a long time, and we faced spiritual warfare all the way, but my mother, father, and siblings are now in the family of God. We're a Muslim family from Deir ez-Zor that loves Jesus!

My healing was the key. How could they deny what had happened? Everyone saw the miracle, and how could they deny the transformation in my life? I used to be negative and caustic, but today, I'm filled with the love of God.

Allahu akbar is Arabic for "God is great! God is great!"

I let Jamila's story sink in. Then the group began worshiping Jesus, and I encouraged them by reading Scripture. We prayed for Jamila and her family. They're believers now, but they're also still refugees. And after years of streaming into the country, displaced Syrians are often despised and rejected. Yet you would never know that by looking at Jamila's joy-filled face.

After a time of prayer focused on Jamila, I turned to another woman.

"Heba, would you share your story?"

Heba's Report on Running to the Light

It all started with my tenderhearted son.

"Momma," he asked me one evening, "why is that building glowing? Can we go in and see?"

Ali was only six years old, but I didn't want to answer his question. The building he wanted to visit was a church, and there was no way I would risk going near a Christian place.

I had a problem, though. The church was in the area where we lived as refugees, and it was right on the main thoroughfare. We could not avoid passing it. And worse, Ali saw the bright light every single time we walked by the church. I couldn't see it, but he would tell me the church was glowing from the inside and was so beautiful. Over and over, he begged me to let him go inside to see it up close.

After putting up with his pleading for days on end, I finally put my foot down.

"Ali," I told him, "we are Muslims, and that building is a Christian church. We don't ever go into a church. It's haram! I will not be seen there for anything. So don't ask me again!"

What I didn't tell Ali was that my biggest fear was his father. What would Hassan think if he knew I was even having this conversation with his little pride and joy?

Ali meant everything to his father. A fervent Sunni Muslim, Hassan dreamed that Ali would become an imam. We had to flee Syria precisely because my husband was such a fanatic. He opposed the Alawite government, and if we had stayed, I would surely have become a widow.

I have to admit that, at times, becoming a widow didn't seem like such a bad idea. My husband was incredibly harsh—more often cruel to me than even the slightest bit loving. But my objection to visiting the church with the light coming out of it did not stop my sweet little son. He kept on begging.

It went on for another month until one day as we were walking down the street, Ali abruptly let go of my hand. He started running, and my heart sank. I knew where he was going, but I couldn't catch him.

When I reached the front door of the church, I could hear the Christians singing inside. Stepping in, I scanned the worshipers for Ali, but he had sat down somewhere, and his tiny body blended in with the crowd. I couldn't find him.

After a few minutes I stopped looking. The words of the music washed over me and drew my heart like a moth to light. It sounded like something from heaven. My feet were rooted to the floor just inside the room, and my mouth gaped involuntarily.

My reaction must have been obvious because a woman came over and said, "Please join me!"

I walked with her to a seat and sat down.

I just sat. And listened. I couldn't move.

After several songs I felt a hand on my shoulder and turned to see Ali standing next to me, an ear-to-ear smile on his precious face. I hugged him and told him I was glad he had run into this place so filled with love.

I could have stayed all day, but after thirty minutes, a pastor stood up and opened the Bible. With all I'd been told about Christian Scriptures being corrupted and altered from their original meaning, I wasn't ready to listen to the man.

Afraid, I scooped Ali under my right arm and told him it was time to go. I thanked the lady who had invited me to sit next to her, and before I could walk away, she kissed me on both cheeks. Then I dashed out the door with Ali.

The singing I heard that day moved my heart and planted in me a longing to know God. I wanted to love Him like the Christians in the glowing church. Their words about Jesus echoed in my mind: "Jesus, name above all names . . ." They called Him beautiful, Savior, and blessed. The living Word.

On the way home Ali told me, "I can't wait to tell Baba all about the singing! I have never seen you smile so much, Momma."

His response to being there was exactly why I hadn't wanted to even peek into the building. If Ali breathed so much as a word of this to his father, I would pay an unbearable price. My mind raced at the horror of what would happen to Ali and me if Hassan heard about our visit to the church.

"Ali," I told him gently, "we'll tell Baba later. But for now, let's keep it our special secret, okay?"

The next Sunday night, Ali and I went for a walk. We had barely gotten out of our apartment when he asked about going to the church. Deep down, I wanted to go. So I thought, *What if we just went in for a couple of minutes this time?* It was dark outside, and the two of us could sneak in, then go to the market just down the street. Hassan would never know.

"Momma, the light is so bright from the church tonight! You see it now, don't you?"

I cringed. Ali spoke loudly, just as we walked by the mosque.

"*Habibi*," I answered, "I don't see the light. I wish I could see what you see, but maybe God has given you special eyes for this . . . this . . . miracle of seeing. It must be supernatural."

I mustered courage as we walked and said to my son, "Ali, we're going to slip in quietly for a few minutes, but you must keep our special secret. We can't tell Baba about this. Promise?"

He responded solemnly, "I promise. I don't think Baba is ready for a church visit. I think he might get angry."

Ali's response caught me off guard. Did he understand more than I thought he did?

Without my asking, he explained.

"I heard Baba talking about Christians, and he said he hates them. He was with some men, and they were saying all the problems in the Middle East are because of Christians. Is that true? Because the people in the shiny building seemed nicer than the people in the mosque. In the church nobody was cranky or angry. Did you notice that?"

"Oh, Ali," I admitted, "I did notice. They were all smiling, weren't they? But we must be careful when talking about this. Shhh!"

I was disappointed that the people weren't singing when we walked in. A man named Osama was speaking from the Isaiah book and the John book. I didn't know there were so many books in the Christian holy Scriptures, and within a few minutes all the things I'd been told about the Bible faded away.

Osama's words were like nothing I'd ever heard before. My icy heart melted in the sunshine of his preaching. The wonder on my face must have been noticeable to others around me.

At this point in Heba's story, a door opened from an office adjacent to the room in which the women's Bible study was meeting, and Pastor Osama walked in. I wondered if the women would wind their hijabs around their heads again to hide themselves from this man, but they didn't. Instead, they smiled and welcomed Osama into the circle. Pastor Osama picked up the story, sharing what he had experienced that night several years earlier.

Pastor Osama's Perspective

Out of the corner of my eye, I saw Heba enter the service. My wife raised her eyebrows and tilted her head toward the door when you walked in, Heba. I got her signal!

You weren't hard to notice in your black abaya and tightly wound hijab, and I immediately adjusted my sermon. Instead of continuing my teaching from Revelation, I began a presentation of the gospel, starting with the words of Isaiah 61 and ending with the gospel of John. I sensed that you and your son truly wanted to be there. In fact, I remember seeing you sit on the edge of your seat. Ali was looking right at me, listening intently.

This is what I said:

> He has come to bring good news to the poor. He has come to bind up the brokenhearted. He has come to set the captives free. He has come to comfort all who mourn. He has come to give you a crown of beauty instead of ashes, the oil of joy instead of mourning. He has come to give you a garment of praise instead of a spirit of despair. He has come to set you free.

He has come to give you life! Come to Jesus,
and everything will change. You will start
your life over and be born again.

For thirty minutes, I preached to Heba and little Ali.
Everyone else at that service was already a believer.
I can still see Heba nodding her head at everything I
said. I could feel excitement in the auditorium because
here among us sat this tightly cloaked woman, obviously
close to salvation. We could see on her face that the
Word of God was touching her deeply, drawing her
heart to His.

People often say that Muslims need to hear the gospel
several times before they're ready to receive Christ. But
why would we say that? God's Word is divinely powerful.
It's living, active, and able to pierce the soul. The name of
Jesus alone can unlock someone's heart.

I, too, had been a Muslim, but the first time I heard
the Bible preached, I knew instantly that it was the Truth.
The Spirit of God convinced me.

So I closed my message, saying, "Let's pray, but
before we do, are there any of you who feel like you're
held captive as Isaiah described? Do you want to be set
free? Jesus wants to forgive your sins. Settle all of this
with Jesus tonight at the cross. Who wants forgiveness
and freedom?"

"I do!" Heba cried out. I think she even shocked herself when she spoke so loudly.

"Then do you remember what happened next,
Heba?" Pastor Osama smiled as he recalled.

Heba's Response

Do I? I'll never forget! First of all, I could not believe that I answered out loud. Had those words really come out of my mouth?

Then the quiet moment was shattered by a shrill voice from a loudspeaker. It was the Muslim call to prayer next door.

I honestly wondered if they had spies in the church to tip them off when the prayer of salvation started. It seemed that the timing couldn't have been a coincidence. Tonight the *muezzin* screeched louder than ever, and for an instant, I was worried.[1] Had they discovered that two Muslims were in the church?

Regardless, that didn't stop the Spirit of God—or my longing to receive Jesus. And I did that night.

I knew I'd better hide my new life in Christ from my fundamentalist husband, so after that, when the call to prayer came each day, I would get down and pray . . . but to Jesus, not to Allah. I'm ashamed to say that I did this for at least a month.

Then one day at Bible study, Naima read a verse written by Paul that says, "I am not ashamed of the gospel of Christ" (Rom. 1:16 KJV).

The message pierced my heart, and I cried. Was I afraid of my husband, or was I ashamed of the gospel? Or was it both?

For sure, I wasn't being truthful with Hassan. I was faking like I was still a Muslim. What must Jesus think? I certainly had let Him down. And what about my son, Ali? I was a terrible example.

Convinced that I must change, the next time the call to prayer sounded, I refused to bow down. Hassan screamed at me, then beat me, insisting that I submit. But I stood strong.

The pattern repeated itself at every call to prayer, and after a time, little Ali had had enough. He tried to defend me, but it was a mistake he never repeated. Hassan turned his wrath on our little boy.

I still shudder when I remember the bruises and swelling. It's by the grace of God that Ali's cheek and nose weren't broken when Hassan punched him full in the face.

Despite the horrors at home, my sisters in Christ were a gift from God when the beatings came five times every day, with each call to prayer. They consoled me whenever I arrived, black and blue. We stood together because they, too, were in difficult, life-threatening situations.

Dalia married an imam, yet she survived. Her threats and beatings were horrible, but she never lost her joy in Christ. And Rima's own son took the house that belonged to her family and threw her out in the cold, yet she remained faithful to Jesus, trusting Him to provide.

The bond we shared was stronger than anything I had ever experienced. We prayed together, studied the Scriptures, and shared our deepest fears and struggles. We also held one another accountable to live as Christ Jesus and obey His words.

The apostle James taught us to be women who are doers of the Word, not merely hearers. As hard as it is to live out your faith in Jesus in a Muslim home, in the strength of the Lord, it is not impossible.

I realized this was a test of my faith. Would Jesus protect me or not?

Hassan's abuse continued, but eventually, he stopped beating me at every call of the muezzin.

Some of my friends could hide their Bibles at home so as to read the precious Word of Life when the coast was clear of abusive husbands, the watching eyes of their sons, or other male relatives. But for a few of us, having a Bible in our possession was not an option. My house consisted of one room that served as both living and sleeping quarters, with one wall as our cooking area. There wasn't a safe place to hide anything of value, let alone a forbidden copy of the Bible.

This drove me to memorize as many verses of Scripture as I could. If I wasn't able to hide God's Word in my home, I would hide it in my heart. And what a gift that ended up being. That way, I could carry it with me everywhere I went, sharing the truth of Jesus with anyone in need.

My mind seemed to soak in every verse. It was as if the Holy Spirit birthed in me a supernatural ability to memorize. I easily remembered whole chapters of the Bible. Eventually, memorizing the Word of God became more important to me than the food I ate. My second passion was teaching God's Word to Ali. He drank in everything I told him about Jesus, and even he could quote an assortment of Bible verses at appropriate times to encourage others.

Now, my greatest prayer is that Hassan will come to know Jesus as Savior.

After each woman finished her remarkable story, each shared passionate pleas for prayer. Many were stunning requests with life-and-death consequences.

Their city is known for its sickening number of honor killings, and the government turns a blind eye to the murder of people just like them. The brutal executions are viewed as a religious right of Muslim families.

I was left wondering, *How can a believer like me from America, a free country, encourage these dear sisters in the faith? What can I say to reinforce their hope?*

Cheeks wet with my own tears, I told these sisters I would never forget them or their life stories. I promised to keep them in my heart and share with others their courage in Christ. I would give them a voice in places they would never visit and encourage as many other followers of Jesus as possible to join me in praying for them. My dream is that the ripple effect of prayer will expand until each one of *their* prayers is answered in an astounding way—for nothing is impossible with God.

I also shared Micah 7:6–8, a scripture the Lord has used to sustain me time and again while I've waited for His answers:

> For a son dishonors his father,
>> a daughter rises up against her mother,
> a daughter-in-law against her mother-in-law—
>> a man's enemies are the members of his own
>> household.

> But as for me, I *watch* in hope for the LORD,
>> I *wait* for God my Savior;
>> my God *will hear* me.

Do not gloat over me, my enemy!
　　Though I have fallen, I will rise.
　　Though I sit in darkness,
　　　　the LORD will be my light. (emphasis added)

I pointed out to my new friends that even though coming to faith in Jesus is not dishonoring to their Muslim family in God's eyes, it feels as if it is to their family members unless they, too, come to believe in Jesus as Savior. And because of the new-birthed faith of these women, their families of origin see them as the enemy. As a result, I told them, "You suffer much at their hands—verbal and physical abuse, persecution, and potentially even death. But never forget the promise of these verses. In spite of your horrific circumstances, you have hope because *God hears you.*

"He hears every single prayer you pray.

"Every time you cry out to Him, He's listening. Every. Single. Time."

What a beautiful promise from the Word of God!

Two hours of stories and Scripture-sharing flew by. Then we prayed—oh, what prayer! Heaven seemed right there in that secured room. The presence of the Lord stunned us into silence, then into praise. It was an hour of prayer so intense I will never forget the feeling.

After long, tender hugs, there was only one thing left to do.

The hijabs went back on. We unbolted the door. And the women of God walked outside into a fanatical, fundamentalist Islamic city to spread the good news of Jesus Christ. Many of them looked back and smiled—their faces reflecting an unshakable faith in Christ.

Answered prayers made them bold. Joy in the Holy Spirit flowed through each of them. And they had one another.

Together, sent by Jesus, they headed back to their mission—extreme, daring, dangerous. Why? Because each of them knows that *every soul matters*. Every abusive husband. Every fanatic imam. Every angry brother. Every mother desperate for what her daughter has found in Jesus.

At times they will dare to speak. But at *all* times they will pray. Because they know heaven and earth will move in response. Will you join them in passionate prayer? Every time you cry out to Him, He's listening.

Every. Single. Time.

> The Lord is near to the brokenhearted
> and saves the crushed in spirit.
>
> Many are the afflictions of the righteous,
> but the Lord delivers him out of them all.
> —Psalm 34:18–19 ESV

CHAPTER 6

TRAPPED IN GAZA

R un to the tent! Everyone!"

An explosion half a block away punctuated Shireen Barghouti's command, and in an instant its shock wave slammed the mother and her four children to the ground.

Her daughter and three sons—all under the age of eight—were screaming as she staggered to her feet. In a desperate attempt at motherly care, she brushed sand from their faces and helped them get up. Resisting panic, Shireen scooped up the two bags of food she had been carrying, and the family of five sprinted through the Deir al-Balah refugee camp.

A second Israeli rocket detonated even closer, once again shoving her and the children onto the dirt road, and Shireen hollered, "We've got to brace ourselves for more air strikes."

She pulled her children close. "I'm sorry to tell you there will be many tonight. But Mommy loves you, and Jesus will keep us safe. He always does. Now, though, we have to get under the mattresses. Come quickly!"

Shireen ran like a mad woman, pulling her children through dusty streets and around piles of garbage. After a terrifying sprint that seemed to last an eternity, they made it to their home—a generic refugee tent among the thousands in their camp.

Once inside, they hunkered on the floor, ready to pull mattresses over their heads, while in the street, a chorus of angry voices began shouting to the rhythm of beating drums. Shireen knew that green-clad Hamas "soldiers," faces covered in black masks and green bandanas plastered with verses from the Qur'an, were now marching past on their way to launch rockets back at Israel.

A protest march at the Gaza fence a few days earlier had triggered a deadly sequence of events. First, a Palestinian gunman fired on two Israeli soldiers, seriously wounding them. Israel responded by killing two well-known terrorists in Gaza. Then Hamas and Islamic Jihad forces fired more than six hundred rockets into the neighboring Jewish state in a barrage that injured nearly one hundred Israelis and killed three.[1]

Knowing it was only a matter of time until Israel responded, Shireen had ventured to the souk to buy food, but she and the children were caught in the open before they could make it home. Compared to some, they were fortunate. That night, Israel's military hit more than 260 sites in Gaza.[2]

"Mommy, is the sky on fire?" five-year-old Jafar wondered.

"That's exactly what it looks like, doesn't it, *habibi*?"

Huddled on the floor, Shireen and her four children braced for a night of no sleep. As usual, she would not have the company of her Muslim husband. He remained in a Hamas prison for being late paying a debt. She would endure the evening's terror alone, yet again.

"It's Jesus and us tonight, children. He will be our guest of honor and will stay here in our tent." Shireen smiled. "Don't you feel privileged? He will never leave us."

The fatherless family drifted in and out of fitful sleep to the sound of explosions, screams, and the grinding of military vehicles.

The next day the Israel Defense Forces (IDF) bombed a car occupied by Hamed Hamdan al-Khodari. The notorious Hamas field commander owned money exchanges through which large sums were imported from Iran to bankroll terrorist activity.[3] His death meant that funding for Hamas and Islamic Jihad would have to find other channels.

In retaliation for al-Khodari's demise, Hamas launched a new round of rockets into Israel. Israel retaliated, of course, and the dismal cycle began again. In the midst of it all, Shireen was living a life she never would have imagined.

TEN YEARS EARLIER

A bomb exploded close—not far from the entrance gate of the refugee camp. Yet despite the ear-shattering blast, not one person in the meeting flinched or even looked up from conversations. Children snuggled a little closer to their moms, but no one paused. It was simply part of life in the Deir al-Balah refugee camp.

Pastor Hanna from a local Gaza church, JoAnn, and I arrived to deliver food packages to refugees but were first required to check in with Abdul, the camp director, at the UNRWA office. (The shortened acronym for the United Nations Relief and Works Agency for Palestine Refugees in the Near East reflects how long the camp has been in operation. No one has referred to this region of the world as the "Near East" since the midtwentieth century.)

Founded in 1948, *Deir al-Balah* means "Monastery of the Dates" because of the abundant date-palm trees indigenous to the area. In the fourth century, during the Byzantine period, a monk built a small hut that grew into a fully functioning Christian sanctuary and guesthouse. But three hundred years later, the upstart religion of Islam rolled in and put an end to the monastery.[4]

Abdul considered himself an inheritor of the Islamic protectorate in the area, yet he was strikingly pleasant, even thanking us for helping his people. He and several of his assistants spoke English and hosted us with hot tea and fresh baklava. All of the men in the small, stuffy trailer wanted their pictures taken with the Americans.

Despite the pleasantries and warm conversation, a collage of photos hanging on the wall defied my best efforts not to stare at them. The men in the photos were a who's who of Gaza terrorists. Abdul made no attempt to hide his background and the network he leveraged to get into his position of responsibility.

"I wanted to be a part of Hamas for years," Abdul said charmingly. "And Allah smiled on me, so . . . well, here I am on this important assignment.

"You know," he continued, "Americans have the wrong idea about Hamas. We are a peaceful group—for the most part. Humanitarian causes are our top priority!

"That's why you're here, is it not? You have a heart for our people, and that is commendable. You are welcome anytime!"

He had distracted me enough from the photos that I could respond. "Thank you, Abdul. JoAnn, Pastor Hanna, and I are grateful for your hospitality. This is too much, really. We appreciate your kindness. Please forgive us for not bringing a gift, but we'd still love to offer you something."

"Sure, you can!" Abdul jumped from his plastic chair with the excitement of a child.

"We want to pray for you and your family, Abdul. And for all the other men here today."

(It's not often you can pray for members of Hamas to meet Jesus, right? How could we miss that opportunity?)

Without giving him a chance to refuse, we launched into a prayer fit for a Billy Graham crusade. The Holy Spirit gave us the words, and each of the men were touched. We could feel it in the room.

Even though these men were involved in a well-known terrorist group—probably sworn enemies of Israel and guilty of heinous crimes—they were human beings created in the image of God. As we have learned from years of working in the Middle East, no one is unreachable. Jesus' love and power can turn even terrorists into some of His most dedicated disciples.

As we concluded our prayer, Abdul had tears in his eyes. He spoke softly.

"That was beautiful. Your words brought comfort to my soul."

Before we could say anything more, he spread his arms wide and gave each of us a giant bear hug. Once released from the embrace, Pastor Hanna was the first to speak.

"Abdul, are we free to go anywhere in the camp and visit the families that have requested help?"

"Of course you are! Stay as long as you want. Most families have never met Americans, so I'm sure you'll draw a crowd. And you are welcome to pray with them just like you did with us." Abdul patted each of us warmly on the back as we left the office.

As soon as we descended the steps from the double-wide trailer, JoAnn recapped the unexpected welcome.

"Pastor Hanna, that was a miracle! A member of Hamas invited us to pray with Muslims in the refugee camp he oversees. Talk about the Holy Spirit invading a place."

It wasn't the only miracle that day.

The conditions in the camp were shocking. At one tent we stared for several seconds at a dead donkey, covered with flies. Suddenly, the donkey moved spastically, in obvious pain. It wasn't quite dead, yet no one cared to help the dying animal or even to put it out of its misery.

We watched flies move from the donkey's bloody face to the children nearby, as they played among piles of garbage. All seemed oblivious to the filth and germs.

Stench from an open sewer fouled the air, but that didn't stop Arab hospitality from being served at every tent we visited. Pastor Hanna translated our prayers for the people we met, and during each prayer, we peeked through our barely parted eyelids, observing the Muslim families. They watched, eyes wide open, as we interceded passionately for them in Jesus' name.

In one dwelling, we met the Baraka family and their ten children. The home was part rusted metal and part worn, dusty black fabric. As we sipped our umpteenth cup of tea for the day, the Barakas talked openly about the hardships of living in Deir al-Balah. The electricity typically was on for no more than one hour a day. Food was scarce, the supply dependent mostly on UNRWA deliveries, plus minimal supplements from the family's odd jobs.

One of their daughters, twenty-year-old Shireen, was a student at Al-Azhar University of Gaza. Excellent in speaking English, Shireen interpreted for her mother as the older woman told her desperate story of sadness and frustration at having lived in the same camp her whole life. When Mrs. Baraka finished, Shireen abruptly offered an account of her own life goals.

"I want to get my college degree, earn a good job, work for about three or four years, and then, someday, buy a laptop computer. That's my dream!"

That's it? I wondered. *Just a computer?*

In our American eyes, her goal was embarrassingly simple. But with unemployment over 40 percent and with 80 percent of the population dependent on aid, we realized in an instant the reasons young people in Gaza aim so low.

Those days in Deir al-Balah changed us, and once we were back in the States, we determined to let the experience influence the message we shared. While speaking at a church in Atlanta, we told Shireen's story, describing the poverty and dangers of Deir al-Balah. We also explained our shock that this dear woman's one and only goal in life was to own a computer.

We could see the effect of our words on the congregation, but we weren't prepared for what happened as a result. At the end of the worship service, a man walked up and handed us a box. In it was a brand-new Toshiba laptop computer he had bought that morning. We looked at the box, then at the man, and wondered if we should be embarrassed.

"We're sorry if you thought we were hinting, as if we were asking someone to give us a computer for Shireen. We didn't mean it that way."

"Oh no, Tom and JoAnn, you didn't ask or even hint. But I've been saving for this, and, man, it's a top-of-the-line, fire-breathing monster of a computer. I haven't even taken it out of the box, and I'm glad I didn't. Because it's as simple as this: When you told Shireen's story, God put four words on my heart, and they kept coming to me over and over. The words were 'Give it to Shireen.'"

Nine months later we were back in Gaza. JoAnn and I headed for Deir al-Balah with the new computer. Abdul gave us directions to the Baraka tent, and off we went.

Shireen and her family could hardly believe we would care to visit them a second time, and we cut straight to the chase about the reason for our visit.

"Shireen, remember the life goal you shared with us last time?"

"I sure do! One day, I pray I can buy a laptop computer." Shireen smiled with pride.

Without a word, JoAnn drew the laptop from behind her back and announced, "Jesus made it happen. It's His gift to you. He wants you to have this, Shireen."

You would have thought we had handed her the keys to a new luxury car. Shireen stared at the box. She didn't—perhaps couldn't—speak a word for at least ten seconds. But then she didn't have to. Her tears spoke of her unspeakable gratitude.

The family gathered around and eyed the computer as if they'd just unearthed a buried treasure. Then a celebration of hugs and endless *shukrans* broke out in that dismal Deir al-Balah tent.[5]

Shireen's computer became a beacon of light in the refugee camp. At the time, 100 percent of the population in Deir al-Balah was Muslim, so we had loaded onto the Toshiba every Christian program we could think of. It hosted the Bible in Arabic and English, worship songs, links to inspirational Bible teaching from Arab churches in the Middle East, and more.

During the electricity hour, Shireen often e-mailed us questions: "Why does Jesus love me?" she asked. "Why do *you* love me?" She also wanted to know things like, "Is Jesus *really* Jewish?"

We shared the gospel with Shireen, but we wondered whether or not she truly understood what we were saying.

A year passed, and we had another opportunity to be in Gaza. We reached out to Shireen via e-mail:

Hey, Shireen, we'll be in Gaza for half a day but at the church that Hanna pastors. It's pretty far from you, though. The service starts at 10:30 a.m. We wish we could see you, but we're sorry we won't have time to get to Deir al-Balah. Next time, okay?

—Tom and JoAnn

We arrived at the church at ten, and as we walked in the front door, we saw Shireen in her black hijab. She and her cousin Fadi (accompanying her to provide the customary male protection) were already seated. They had been the first ones there.

When the worship started, Shireen sang loudly, a broad smile on her face. To say we were surprised she knew the words would be an understatement. She nodded her head enthusiastically when she found out I would be preaching.

As for us, wow! Two Muslims were sitting in a church in Gaza. I changed the sermon on the spot and packed it with the gospel.

After finishing, I sat down next to Shireen. With her fist, she popped me playfully in the ribs and blurted, "Good job, Tom Doyle."

Her open display surprised us—especially that she would offer a positive response to the sermon from the Bible with her cousin sitting right next to her. To my amazement, though, he nodded in agreement.

"You liked the Bible message, Shireen?" I asked after I picked my jaw up off the floor.

"Well, of course I did! Because I have Jesus in my heart now. Didn't you know that, Tom?"

Double wow! We *didn't* know it, and right out of the chute, Shireen told us that she was the first believer in the Deir al-Balah refugee camp.

"We have to spread the word about Jesus in Deir al-Balah!" Shireen quivered excitedly under her hijab as she told me about her new life goal. "Many people are open minded and would love to learn about Jesus."

Dozens of fellow believers hugged Shireen before we left, and her cousin even seemed to enjoy the attention.

It's amazing what God can use for His purposes.

A glass of water.

A kind word.

A small gift.

A Jesus dream.

Or a computer . . . to reach the first-ever believer in a Muslim refugee camp.

But the Word of God is the centerpiece of His power. The eternal words from the God of heaven transform the human heart.

Shireen could not "recover" from reading the Bible for the first time. She was undone and gave her life to Christ without hesitation. Today she loves Jesus and is a rare voice for Truth in Gaza.

TRAPPED BUT FAITHFUL

Shireen Baraka Barghouti lives in a cauldron of hate that often boils over. She's never been outside the Gaza Strip even though it's only twenty-five miles long and three miles wide at the narrowest borders, seven miles at the widest.

Qasem Soleimani, until his death in 2020, was the major general over Iran's Islamic Revolutionary Guard Corps (IRGC), who invested monstrous sums of Iranian money in the youth of Gaza. In fact, Hamas simply could not exist without the Iranian money he supplied. And to make sure he covered all the bases, Soleimani also funded the rival Islamic Jihad. Shireen doesn't hold back when speaking about the climate of death and destruction that has helped create.

"In Gaza, *terrorism* is our number-one export," she said.

"How sad that whenever the Gaza Strip is mentioned, people automatically think of radical Islamic terrorists. But how could they not? Our Gaza government is run by them. Iran gives Hamas thirty million dollars *a month*.

"At different times we've had al-Qaeda, the Islamic State, the Muslim Brotherhood, and the Popular Front for the Liberation of Palestine in charge, to name just a few. New groups form every year, and our young Gaza boys see these 'freedom fighters' as heroes to emulate.

"In Europe, people idolize soccer players. But not in Gaza. Here, men dressed in green uniforms, toting AK-47s, and shouting 'death to Israel' are featured on billboards.

"The explosions are enough to cause you a nervous breakdown. A few years ago Hamas fired over ten thousand rockets into Israel in one extended attack over several months. We knew it was just a matter of time before the Israelis responded, and once we heard the drones humming over Gaza, we took cover.

"Hamas has done nothing for the people of Gaza. While they line their pockets with millions of dollars, the people go without eating. They are cruel and intentionally keep us in this senseless war with Israel.

"You might think because I live in Gaza and grew up Muslim that I hate Israel. But I don't. I do detest Hamas, however—and all the other terrorist groups that make life unbearable in the Strip.

"I'm raising four children here. Three are boys, and I wonder, *What kind of a future do they have?*"

Her question is a good one. In May 2019, expert bomb maker Fadi Abu al-Sabah secured a humanitarian visa into Israel.

His motives were anything but concern to help people in need. Hamas had sent al-Sabah to establish terror cells in the West Bank, but the terrorist explosives expert was arrested by Israel in Taybeh.[6]

Why is this significant? Because Fadi Abu al-Sabah had been a resident of the Nuseirat refugee camp. This is the kind of neighborhood Shireen lives in.

Since 1948, Gaza's eight refugee camps have been a breeding ground for terrorism. Yet there is no good reason for even one camp to exist. Although Gaza is densely populated, there is plenty of room to build houses—if Hamas cared to.

Keeping Palestinians in refugee camps supports the narrative that Israel is responsible for the mess. Hamas and other terrorist groups get rich by remaining a thorn in Israel's side and by manipulating their own people for the "cause."

To be sure, Israel has not been perfect in their treatment of Palestinians, and Gaza has been their ultimate challenge. Rooting out terrorists in crowded civilian areas is extremely demanding—and ultimately unrealistic. The result is the continuing needless and heartbreaking loss of innocent lives in the Strip.

Shireen Explains the Misery Cycle in Gaza

Here's how it goes in Gaza.

The Hamas government eventually gets to the point where the people are disgusted with their hardline rule and want to throw them out. They become desperate enough to try the impossible. Recently, there have been protest marches against Hamas here in Gaza, and the people were not killed. This is a first.

Hamas is evil, but they're not stupid. They can sense when the people are at a breaking point and when their approval rating is in the tank. So what's their solution? They attack Israel, of course—with thousands of missiles. They bait the Israelis into a war until their military invades Gaza. That's when it gets really ugly, all over again.

Can you imagine raising a family in this? A mother innately has hope for the future of each child the Lord gives her. But reality dashes that hope to the ground when there is no escaping the poverty, squalid living conditions, and war.

In Gaza, I spent much of my time dreaming about what life could be like on the other side of the fence, free from this darkness and hatred.

Just recently, we had no food for several days. Like so many in the Strip, my husband had no work before he went to prison for not being able to pay our bills. Our children cried and went to school hungry, day after day. My heart broke more than I ever thought it could.

So how can a mother think about anything other than just getting out of Gaza and giving her children a better life? It's tempting to base our lives here solely on what we are hoping for. We live for tomorrow but forget the importance of today.

For a long while I obsessed over this and lived often in a fantasy world: how I would give anything just to take our four children to a church. But I could never do that in Gaza. The time I went to the church in Gaza to meet Tom was beautiful and uplifting. But if I did this continually and was spotted by fundamentalist Muslims, I would be killed, and my children raised by Muslim relatives.

So to answer my own question: How can a mother think about anything other than just getting out of Gaza and giving her children a better life? Jesus showed me how to do it. He taught me to *fix my eyes on Him* and not the things around me. So now, my focus is on Him, and I'm called to be faithful in the Gaza Strip. Someday, I may get asylum and be able to leave. Then again, I may not.

But, whatever happens, *Jesus has called me to be a woman of God in the Gaza Strip.* I am needed here and have a special assignment from God. My younger sister loves Jesus now, and we pray together and share Bible verses. I also tell others how to find eternal life in Jesus—here in this place known for death.

I still wear a hijab and an abaya because I'm an underground believer for Christ. If I did not have children, I would come out openly and tell everyone in the Deir al-Balah refugee camp. I would no doubt be persecuted and probably killed, but I love Jesus that much. Besides protecting my children, though, I also want to reach the rest of my family.

My husband will be released from prison soon. His family is a strict, observant Muslim clan, and our marriage was not one based on love. He has not ever bought me a present for a birthday or anniversary. And I confess to you that I dreamed of leaving him.

I believe, though, that Jesus can breathe life back into a marriage. Look at what He did with Dina and Mohammad in Lebanon. I'm praying for a miracle like that! The good news is that my husband has seen the changes in my life, and he is opening up to Jesus. Sometimes, the hardest people to reach for Christ are in our own families. So I ask you: Will you pray for him?

Whatever your situation in life is, remember this: embrace life and be faithful to Jesus. He has been and will always be faithful to you. Your life might not be what you hoped for, and it might not have turned out like you planned. Yet He wants you to be a flower that grows out of the dirt to reflect His glory.

That growth, though, will never happen if you focus your thoughts on what you *don't* have. Fix your eyes on Jesus! He is the Author and Perfecter of our faith [Heb. 12:2].

Pray for change, pray for miracles, but don't let your faith get paralyzed when things don't happen on your schedule. Jesus is faithful. If you fix your eyes on Him, the problems and challenges in this life will pale in comparison.

I know this to be true because I've seen it work in my life as a woman for Christ in Gaza. I pray for you, my dear friends in Christ. I pray you will remember me and pray for me in the Deir al-Balah refugee camp. The word on the street is that Hamas will launch another major battle with Israel soon, and the people of Gaza will suffer even more.

I try not to think of these things. I choose to fix my eyes on Jesus Christ.

But you, O LORD, are a shield about me,
   my glory, and the lifter of my head.
I cried aloud to the LORD,
   and he answered me from his holy hill.

   —PSALM 3:3–4 ESV

CHAPTER 7

THE GREAT
MECCA ESCAPE

Khadija Qureshi had done this more times than she could count, but every time she stood at the entrance of *al-Masjid al-Haram*, the thrill nearly overwhelmed her.[1] Once again she relished being among more than two million faithful Muslims in Mecca—her hometown—for the annual *hajj*.[2] The mass of humanity had begun the counterclockwise walk she was so familiar with.

Named for one of Muhammad's wives, Khadija—"Kady," as her friends knew her—took a deep breath. *Only the faithful are here*, she mused. *Infidels discovered here will die*.

Kady exhaled slowly and entered the line to begin her journey. Satisfaction and joy flooded her soul. She could hardly fathom the path that had brought her to this old, familiar place in such an exciting, new way. She shivered in anticipation of the long, slow walk around the Kaaba stone and hoped it would not be her last.[3]

But this was the *first time* Kady came to pray for others at Islam's holiest site . . . as a new follower of Jesus.

TEN MONTHS EARLIER

Two twentysomething women in black hijabs huddled at a corner table at their favorite meeting spot in the Strawberry and Cheese bakery. It was a place where the only secrets were the ones the two besties kept from the rest of the world.

Friends from their days as children, they knew everything about each other. And here in their safe place, no conversation was out of bounds. How many boys had they scrutinized together? What were their most recent family foibles? Their latest hopes for the future? They talked of their heartbreaks, of dreams that so many times seemed impossible, and of religion, of course. Kady and Amina were as close as sisters. Still, no past conversation or deep, personal revelation had prepared Amina for the story her friend shared this time.

Kady raised a caramel macchiato to her lips, sipped the drink, then leaned into the table toward her friend.

"Jesus came to Mecca."

At first the words didn't register with Amina, and she stared blankly at her friend, who had just returned from the annual hajj.

Kady returned the stare, her eyes serious but calm. "And I wasn't the only one who saw Him."

Amina sat back slowly and raised her coffee cup in front

of her face, an unconscious motion to protect herself from her friend's scandalous words. But Kady continued.

"*I* saw Him, Amina. Jesus was there in a white robe." Kady shook her head almost imperceptibly. "I will never forget the light that flowed from Him."

She breathed the words, then paused, eyeing her friend. After several seconds, a bare smile tugged at the corners of her mouth.

"Let's go to the Kaaba, and I'll show you where I saw Him. It's only a fifteen-minute cab ride."

"Kady!" Amina's eyes flared. "Calm down. Has my *habibti* lost her mind? Have you forgotten where we live? We're in *Mecca*. You can't talk openly like this. Not if you know what's good for you."

DARE TO ASK

Amina glanced around the café, then focused on Kady.

"We've been best friends since the first grade, Kady. And I admit I've never had the passion for Islam you've had. You were on fire for our religion." Amina tapped her own chest. "As for me, I've just seen too many disturbing things that made me question, question, question.

"The whole treatment of women in Islam is a problem for me too big to swallow. Do women even matter to Allah? Does he care about us at all? If we're descendants of Ishmael, then why is it that his mother, Hagar, is not named even once in the Qur'an?" She pointed an index finger at Kady. "Why didn't Allah ever say her name? Sure, she's alluded to, but there's no honor in that. Why was she never mentioned?

"I don't think Allah even hears us. Nothing I've *ever* prayed for was answered by him." Her words became a rant. "I feel like I'm invisible, Kady. No one seems to notice me except you, my friend.

"And why am I even talking about how I feel about myself and our religion to you, anyway? You've changed. You're so different." The words trailed off.

Kady sat quietly, knowing her friend had more to say.

"After being a practicing Muslim your whole life and preaching to me . . . now all of a sudden, you're talking to me about Jesus? Like He might be *more* than just one of the prophets."

Amina waved her hands across the table. "What's gotten into you? Do your parents know about this yet?"

Kady smiled at the question.

"Amina, I long for the day I tell them about Jesus." She paused. "I asked Jesus for a sign because I was having so many dreams about Him. In each dream He would tell me words that pierced my heart. *Kady,* He said, *Remember this: I love you, and I will never leave you.*

"So I prayed one night, 'Jesus if You're who You say You are . . . meet me at the Kaaba stone during the hajj.'

"I was in the sacred house, on my first walk around the stone. And all of a sudden, I heard it. I was concentrating on my prayers when the name *Jesus* pierced through my memorized words, and I said His name out loud.

"But it wasn't just me who said His name. I realized people around me all uttered it at the same time. How could that be? I immediately wondered if the chief executioner was notified. But no one moved, and no one infiltrated the mass of people. A few minutes later I heard it again. Was it just me? Others too?

"I found out later that a whole group of people had a vision of Jesus at the same time." Kady shook her head. "I still don't know how He could do that. But there He was! We saw Jesus standing on top of the Kaaba stone with an astounding, magnetic smile on His face. Instinctively, I reached for Him. Then I was instantly afraid and drew my hands back. What if someone saw me?

"But I stared at Jesus, and He seemed to sense my fear. He did not want me to be frightened and swept His hand over the mass of people for me to see what was happening.

"I realized I wasn't alone. So many hands were reaching toward Him, Amina. I had no doubt—He was there. Jesus was there—at the *Kaaba!*"

Kady gave her friend several seconds to absorb what she had shared; then she spoke the most startling words Amina had ever heard: "A short while later I gave my life to Jesus—and it was the best decision I've ever made."

Amina stood abruptly and grabbed her friend by the arm. "Let's go for a walk."

Once outside, Amina got in Kady's face.

"When you told me just now your story about Jesus at the Kaaba and that others saw Him, I got chills all over." Her eyes drilled into Kady. "I'm an accountant, and I don't have the emotional nature you do. But what you just told me . . ." She blinked hard, then added as blandly as she could. "It warmed my heart."

Amina stood facing her friend and took several deep breaths. "Do you think Jesus would ever come to me in a dream?"

Kady beamed and bear-hugged Amina. "I'll pray that He does, Amina!"

"Shush, Kady. You've got to tone it down. You're talking so loud, people will think you're an American Christian!"

"I know. I do need to be more careful. I'm still figuring all of this out, Amina."

Kady looped her right arm around Amina's elbow, and the two walked arm in arm down the street. A block into their stroll, Kady spoke again.

"So even though you're disappointed with Allah, do you still pray, Amina? I know you used to."

Amina adjusted her head covering as if to show she was religious. Kady could see that her friend was offended by the question.

"Of course, I pray, Kady! I do because I . . . am supposed to. Well, anyway, I mean sometimes I pray." She scowled at her friend. "That's kind of personal, you know. What are you doing? Checking up on me or something? Are you training to be a *mutawa*?"[4]

The two women laughed.

"Amina, since when are we *not* personal? You and me— no secrets, remember? The reason I asked you about praying is because I know I can't point to a single prayer that Allah ever answered either—ever. And you just said that he hasn't answered any of your prayers. Is he even listening? I don't think so.

"I mean, I have poured my heart out at the Kaaba and spilled buckets of tears. And what did he do? He did *nothing*, Amina. Absolutely nothing!"

Kady Qureshi took a deep breath, steadied herself, and planned her next words.

"Here's what I know to be true, Amina: Jesus answers prayer; Allah does not."

Kady's best friend stopped walking and stared into the sky, a pained expression on her face. Without looking down, she spoke coldly.

"First of all, talking like that, my friend, could get you a prison sentence. There is no room for exploring spiritual things outside of Islam while you're inside the Kingdom."

Amina then looked down at the pavement and whispered, "You're right, though. I go through the motions in prayer, but in my heart, I stopped praying years ago. Allah doesn't hear anything I say. To him, I'm invisible. It's like I don't exist."

After the confession Amina pulled Kady into a hug, and tears fell onto the Jesus follower's shoulder. After several seconds Kady took Amina by the shoulders.

"My question wasn't meant to make you feel guilty. We both know there's enough of that to go around in our religion. My point is this: when I started praying to Jesus, every time I asked for something, He answered.

"Every. Single. Time."

Kady paused, an idea forming. "Ask Him for something, Amina." She smiled impishly. "I dare you!"

Amina sneered. "Kady, Jesus wouldn't answer my prayer. I don't believe in Him like you do. Besides, I think you're imagining all this anyway." She stopped, looked at the pavement, then up at her friend. "Are you actually daring me to ask Jesus for something?"

Kady nodded slowly, smugly. "Yeah, Amina. Yeah . . . it's an official dare!"

Amina nodded back. "Wow. You are the pushy girl! And . . . okay. Since you dared me, here's my request: Jesus, if You're real, then come to me in a dream *tonight*—just like You appeared to Kady. That is, if You ever really did that in the first place." Amina smirked. "How was that for a prayer, Kady?"

"Well, it's a start, *habibti*. I'm not sure you actually expect Jesus to answer you, but . . . at least you prayed! Talk tomorrow?"

"Yes, and if your phone rings in the middle of the night, you'll know your Jesus came to me." Amina laughed out loud. "Like that would ever happen. I can't believe I took this dare, Kady! It's not like me to even care about all this religious stuff anymore."

Kady smiled, shook her head, and gave her friend the "Oh, Amina!" look.

"My phone will be on the nightstand. I'll be waiting to talk to you."

The two women hugged, then turned to walk their separate ways. Kady did a wiggle dance under her abaya and glanced back at Amina with a laugh. Kady held up her phone and sent Amina a text: **Call me after He visits you tonight!**

At seven the next morning Kady woke up and started the day with a sigh. She realized immediately that she had not heard from Amina overnight.

She rose slowly from bed and stumbled downstairs for breakfast. As she entered the kitchen, her mom and dad greeted her in unison.

"*Sabah alkhyr*, Kady!"[5]

Basima Qureshi pulled out a chair from the breakfast table for her youngest daughter.

"Kady, what got into you last night? You could've slept through a war. You were so tired. Are you okay?"

Kady was bewildered. "I slept well?"

"Yes, you did. Amina just called me and said she's been trying to reach you all night. You girls amaze me at how you talk to each other, sometimes at three in the morning! She said something about having a crazy dream. What's that about? Did you forget to charge your phone again, sweetie?"

Kady jumped from her chair and grabbed her mother's phone.

"Can I make a quick call, Mom?"

Basima nodded, even though her daughter had already dialed.

"Amina! I'm sorry I missed your call." Kady's tight grip on the phone inadvertently switched on the speaker.

"My call?" Amina said with a heavy dose of sarcasm. "My *calls*, you mean. From one until five in the morning I dialed, I texted. I was ready to walk to your house and throw a rock at your window.

"He came, Kady. He really did!"

Kady's mom, intrigued by the conversation being broadcast across the kitchen, joined in.

"*Who* came? Who came, Amina? Did a relative surprise you?"

"*Sabah alkhyr* to my second mom!" Amina shouted.

"No need to shout, Amina. Look who's talking loudly now." Kady's face contorted humorously. "Whoops! I had it on speaker."

"So who came to see you, Amina?" Basima pressed.

"A new Friend visited me last night."

"Oh . . . well . . . I hope if it was a man . . . I hope your parents were aware someone came to see you." Basima raised her eyebrows.

"No worries there," Amina said in a calming tone. "My parents were home. Thank you for always looking out for me, Basima. I love you!"

Kady nodded coyly at her mom, clicked off the speaker, and exited the kitchen. As Kady climbed the stairs to her bedroom, Amina continued.

"Boy, Kady, you're really blowing it all over the place. First, you don't answer my calls or texts, and then you put our conversation on speaker so your whole family can hear it. Nice going."

"You're right. I'm a mess for some reason." Kady shrugged as she laughed. "Meet at Strawberry and Cheese bakery at nine?"

AMINA WAKES UP

Kady was on her second caramel macchiato, and for one of the rare times in her life, the chatty young woman was speechless. The only time she opened her mouth while Amina described her Jesus dream was to sip her coffee.

"Kady, here's what Jesus said to me last night, the best night of my life: *Amina, I am* El Roi, *the God who sees you. That is My name. That is who I am. I hear your cries. I hear you, and I see you, Amina.*

"He told me that He loves me! I hung on every word and didn't want Him to leave." Amina closed her eyes briefly, relishing the memory of her dream. "Do you think He will come visit me again?

"Jesus *sees* me, Kady. He loves me!"

Excitement overflowing, Kady jumped out of her chair and leaned over their corner table toward Amina.

"I knew He would come to you! Even though you were a doubting Thomas for sure."

"What's a 'doubting Thomas,' Kady? I've never heard that phrase."

"That's about to change, Amina. Tonight, you and I are going to one of my favorite places."

"We are?"

"Yes, my friend. We're going to the Well." Kady's eyes sparkled.

Amina stood up and shrugged, her face reflecting the confusion in her thoughts.

"Do you mean a well in the desert? Are you talking about the Zamzam well? The one Allah provided for Ishmael?"

"Not that one, Amina, but don't worry. This well is like none you've ever been to. I'm sure of that. We can walk there from your apartment. See you at eight o'clock, okay?"

This time it was Amina who did a wiggle dance under her abaya as she skipped out of the café.

At eight o'clock sharp Amina and Kady stepped onto the sidewalk outside Amina's apartment. They walked several blocks before turning onto a side street. Kady led Amina in a series of right-left turns through another half-dozen blocks before making a U-turn. In the middle of another block, they turned into a modest apartment building.

Near the top of a third flight of stairs, Amina grabbed Kady by the arm. "I thought we were going to the Well." She pointed up the last few steps. "Whose apartment is this?"

"This is where the Well meets tonight, Amina. It's the safest place. Wait here, okay?"

Kady walked up the remaining steps and delivered several purposefully short knocks on the apartment door. She counted to ten, then spoke three words loud enough for anyone inside the apartment to hear.

"Go Real Madrid!"

Amina's eyes widened as she realized her friend had just uttered some sort of password. The door opened quickly.

"Come in, Kady! The game is going to be a good one tonight. Real Madrid versus Barcelona! You better be for Real Madrid, my friend."

As Amina followed Kady into the apartment, she startled to see nearly two dozen men and women in their twenties and thirties sitting on the floor and a soccer game playing on a TV against the far wall.

The man who had let them in shut the door, locked it, and introduced himself to Amina. Ziad then motioned toward the group. Kady introduced Amina, triggering a series of questions from the alleged soccer fans.

"So, Amina, are you a seeker?"

"What brings you here?"

"Did you have a Jesus dream?"

Finally, one woman explained, "Kady told us about you."

Amina bristled. "Oh, she did, did she? Well, I have a question for you. Are we going to watch a soccer game? Because Kady told me . . ."

Ziad cut her off with a laugh. "No, Amina, the game is just for cover. We're here to worship Jesus. But since we live in Mecca, any kind of meeting like this could get us killed. No one cares if we watch soccer, though, so the game stays on."

Ziad al-Jihad pulled a Samsung Galaxy S10 out of his back pocket and waved it at the gathering. In response, a hand near the television reached out and turned up the volume while the group formed a tight circle on the floor.

Ziad spoke one sentence: "The Holy Spirit put this strongly on my heart for us to read together tonight."

Phones lit up, and Ziad signaled: *left fist, one finger, sixteen fingers.* Without speaking, twenty-two people turned to the Old Testament, book of Genesis, chapter sixteen. A meeting of Mecca's underground church was now in session.

Each person read the chapter on their phone. Amina leaned close to Kady and read from her phone. After several minutes the "congregation" had finished reading the chapter, and each person began to talk quietly with the people closest to them.

Kady spoke softly to Amina, barely audible: "In this chapter, I learned that Hagar was alone in the desert—a despised woman with nowhere to go. But the Lord *saw* her. He *heard* her." She whispered in Amina's ear, "In the Old Testament, the 'Angel of the Lord' means a visit from Jesus."

Kady pointed to the words on her phone screen. "See, He even allowed Hagar to give Him a name: 'You are the God who sees me' [v. 13]. She called Him that."

Kady hugged her lifelong friend and asked, "So, Amina, what did you learn from Genesis 16?"

Amina stared straight ahead for several seconds, then leaned into Kady and began to cry.

"I'm overwhelmed to be here! First, I had the dream about Jesus, and now I'm here with all these people who love one another like family. My heart has never felt so full, Kady."

She slowly shook her head in wonder. "So what I learned is this: Because I am a Muslim, I am a daughter of Hagar. Not only did Jesus come to her; He came to *me*. We both wondered if God was seeing us. And He does see us, Kady. We're women, yet He sees us . . . and loves us." She paused before continuing. "In the Qur'an, Allah does not even say Hagar's name, but in the Bible, Hagar is honored and loved and was even privileged to give God one of His names. Can you believe it? My mind just can't comprehend all of this. I'm so relieved! How wonderful that Jesus loves us."

When the whispers died down, singing began—underground-church singing. The assembly mouthed words to each hymn but did not sing out loud. Amina surveyed the room. Smiling faces read the words on their phones. The group was in perfect sync, their worship focused on Jesus.

In their hearts the believers sang at the top of their lungs. The words just never made it past their lips. The neighbors had no idea what was happening among the soccer fans, but *Jesus was being exalted in Mecca.* Amina joined in with a passion Kady had never seen in her singing. "You're a good, good Father."

A number of worshipers began to cry at the tangible presence of the Lord. Ziad sent a telephone message to pause the worship, then turned and whispered to Bassem next to him. Bassem then whispered a message to the man on the other side of him, who in turn began a series of message passing until the whisper reached Amina. When she heard Ziad's words, Amina began to cry like a newborn.

Well practiced at covering emotional moments, the Well went into full security mode and began to clap and cheer for Real Madrid to make sure the neighbors didn't hear Amina's sobs.

A few minutes later, through her tears, Amina passed the message to Kady: "The name Hagar gave to God in Hebrew—*El Roi, the God who sees you*—is the beautiful name she chose."

Then Amina added her own commentary. "Kady, that's exactly what Jesus said to me in my dream. He said, *Amina, I am El Roi, the God who sees you. That is My name. That is who I am. I hear your cries. I hear you, and I see you, Amina.* Then Jesus told me He loved me. How could it be, Kady, that the very first time I read the Bible, it answered my deepest questions? Not only that, but the words Jesus said to me in my dream are the very ones we read tonight. This is too big to ignore and certainly can't be a coincidence."

Kady and Amina embraced, tears flowing.

Kady whispered in her friend's ear: "He came to you, Amina. He sees you. Even when you didn't believe He would, Jesus honored your prayer. You prayed one time, and Jesus did all of this for you."

"Oh, Kady, I've never felt so much love in a room of people in my life. Men and women worshiping Jesus together!"

Two hours later Amina asked Kady to pray with her to receive Jesus as Savior, and twenty-two sets of hands rested on Amina as she sobbed her way through the prayer.

DAUGHTERS OF THE KING— LIVING IN MECCA

For several months Kady and Amina met with the Well every week at a different apartment. Their congregation was among a network of fifteen (and growing) secret churches meeting in Islam's holiest city. Along with their belief in Christ, the groups held security procedures in common. After reading the Bible on their phones, each participant hit an app that performed a daily "screen replacement" to hide the incriminating words.

For additional fellowship Amina and Kady took walks at lunchtime from the Jabal Omar Hyatt Regency Makkah, where they both worked. Since the hotel was across the street from the

Great Mosque of Mecca, they stayed on the alert for "listening ears" and spoke in code about what they were studying in the Bible. Later, when they knew it was safe, they would each look up the other's Scripture passage.

In one exchange, for instance, they discussed a gospel passage: "*Jamal* told me to tell you His *exciting news*. He *e-mailed me at four* and told me the *crops are ready to be picked*."

Their coded message really meant: *Jesus* told me to tell you from the *gospels, in John chapter four,* "Lift up your eyes, and see that the *fields are white* for harvest" [v. 35 ESV, emphasis added].

"Amina, I think something historic is coming to Mecca. A bumper crop is on the way! The fields are white just like Jamal said."

For six weeks after the exchange, Kady and Amina walked and prayed together around the Great Mosque. They asked God to raise up millions to pray for Muslims during the hajj. They also asked that God burn into the hearts of Muslim-background believers to come to Mecca and pray during the pilgrimage week.

On one of their walks Amina checked, then double-checked for people who might overhear before she asked Kady, "Have you ever thought about how Muslim countries actually help us spread the gospel of Jesus? Our passports say 'Muslim,' which means we believers can come to Mecca and pray during hajj, and no one knows the difference. No one else has our free pass. If we didn't live in an Islamic country, it wouldn't be possible. Wouldn't it be great if one hundred MBBs came to pray this year?"

Kady's eyes widened. "Amina, you're right! Let's pray for believers all over the Muslim world to have the courage to come to Mecca for intensive prayer during hajj." She eyed her friend. "Will you be there with me?"

Amina smiled. Kady already knew the answer to her question. "I wouldn't miss it for anything!"

BRAVE NEW WORLD

The night before the big event, the Well met for prayer, and all twenty-two participants committed to be at the hajj. They would pray there for breakthroughs in the Muslim world. The whisper prayer session that night was electric.

Back at home, as Kady was getting ready for bed, Basima stopped by her daughter's room.

"Going to the first day tomorrow?"

Kady smiled pleasantly at her mother. "Wouldn't miss it for anything, Mom."

Kady arrived at the hajj along with Amina, Ziad, and the rest of the Well, but the group split up and entered at different intervals so as to spread out their prayer coverage. The goal was simple: they would pray for every person they laid eyes on.

Lord, get Your Word to all of these people who desperately need You.

Jesus, meet this man in his dreams.

Jesus, show this woman truth.

Father, draw these lost souls to You. This one, Father, and that one . . .

This man in a wheelchair, heal him for Your glory, Lord.

Reveal Your holiness to each lost soul, my Savior.

Each of them knew that if a Christ follower was discovered at the hajj, the believer would be beheaded. But Kady and Amina prayed for one hundred MBBs to risk it all, journey to Mecca, and pray during the hajj. What they hadn't anticipated was that their prayer was too small for God.

The Well was not on its own at the Great Mosque, and Kady was not the only prayer warrior to survive her first-ever time at the Kaaba walk as a believer in Christ. Later, she and Amina discovered that more than six thousand believers had prayed that year at the hajj.

A HOUSE DIVIDED

After finding out through the underground-church network that Mecca had hosted thousands of secret believers, Kady was on a spiritual high. She couldn't stop thinking about how stunning it was that God had embedded believers in the midst of two million Muslim pilgrims circling the Kaaba. He had fielded a prayer *battalion* for Jesus.

Inspired by the Spirit's movement at the hajj, Kady believed that God would answer even more prayers for Muslims to embrace Jesus. On a lunch walk shortly after the hajj, Kady spelled out a daring plan to Amina.

"It's time to start planting seeds. I can't bear the thought that one day my entire Qureshi family will spend eternity separated from God. I'm asking Jesus to break through the spirit of Islam and save their souls. Pray for me tonight. I'm going to talk to them." She eyed Amina with resolve. "I'm not afraid."

A typical, observant—and extremely wealthy—Muslim family in Mecca, the Qureshis met every external criteria of good Muslims. But like most people living in the spiritual center of Islam, they considered life in Mecca a nuisance. The traffic caused by two million visitors a year motivated even the most fervent Muslims to yearn for a more peaceful existence in the deserts of the Kingdom. Still, the mystique of Islam's ancient roots had tethered the Qureshi family to Mecca for generations. They couldn't imagine living any other place than the spiritual epicenter of the religion they were so proud of.

The Qureshi clan also enjoyed status in Mecca. The long line of religious clerics in the family and wealthy business owners were part of the fabric of the local culture. So despite her inner preparation since talking at lunch with Amina, Kady shocked herself with the question she asked openly at the family dinner that night.

"Mom and Dad, do you ever wonder if Allah is listening to you?"

It was bad enough that she had missed Friday prayers that day, so when Kady asked her question, the room fell starkly silent for nearly a minute. The question lit a fire in the eyes of Wahhab and Khaled, her two older brothers, but her father spoke first.

"What do you mean, *Is Allah listening to us?*" Kareem Qureshi began speaking softly, but his voice rapidly escalated in volume. "Kady, we live in the city that fellow Muslims flock to because it is *the* holy place. Allah answers all our prayers here. How dare you even ask that question!"

Kareem's quick rage at his daughter rendered the rest of the evening awkward. Little more was said, and after dessert Kady feared the worst when Wahhab and Khaled slipped quietly out the back door.

Later that week the Well was in celebration mode when the last of the expected secret knocks sounded. Amina arrived after working late and hadn't noticed the uninvited visitor who followed her into Ziad's apartment.

"Marhaba! Can I come to the party too?"

The voice behind her was louder than any regular group member would use for a greeting, and in the split second before Amina could turn around, she realized two things: the voice was familiar, and Kady, who was looking at her from Ziad's living room, had turned white with panic. Ziad, though, didn't flinch as the voice spoke to him.

"I'm Khaled Qureshi, and you are?"

"Ziad al-Jihad." The host smiled. "Marhaba! Come join this party, brother. I hope you like soccer. Are you related to Kady over there?"

Before Khaled could answer, his younger sister recovered, lunged across the room, and hugged her brother. He was there to spy on her, but Ziad's coolheaded response helped her put on a good front.

"Khaled, I'm surprised you're here, but I'm glad you came. You're going to feel right at home, big brother. Real Madrid rules this apartment, and the game is on in ten minutes."

Suspicious, Khaled measured his sister. "I've discovered something new about my sister tonight: she is a soccer fan! When did this happen, Kady?"

"I was surprised, too, Khaled, but I've gotten caught up in the games lately. Karim Benzema is my favorite. What an athlete!" She pointed to their host. "Ziad is a Sergio Ramos fan." She looked charmingly at her brother. "Can you believe the kind of money they make, Khaled?"

The group picked up Khaled's obvious ulterior motives and focused on nothing but the game while he sat silently among them. Kady's brother stayed for half the game and then left, offering an excuse that he had to attend another meeting.

Amina slipped into another room and watched through barely parted curtains as Khaled made a phone call from his car. He talked for several minutes, and once he drove away, Amina told the group the coast was clear. Ziad and the others huddled close in the living room.

"Kady, your brother suspects you, and I'm sorry to say I sensed a spirit of evil in the room when he was here. Is your computer clean?"

"Yes, nothing is on my computer. I followed security protocol." Kady was unnerved but sure of herself.

"Well, he's onto you." Ziad paused, then continued with sadness in his voice. "If your family found out you gave your life to Jesus and that you left Islam, do you have any reason to think they would try to kill you?"

Kady took a long, deep breath and stared at the ceiling to gather her thoughts.

"I had dreams of leading my family to Jesus, but who am I kidding? We live in Mecca, and my family is well known. Many of my cousins and uncles are Muslim clerics."

She paused, then looked Ziad in the eye. "Yes. They would kill me. Or they would give my name to Muhammad Saad al-Beshi. I hear he's one of Mecca's top executioners now. What an honor that would be, right?"

Kady smiled wryly. "Have you seen al-Beshi's latest interview?

He bragged about how proud he is to do God's work and doesn't lose any sleep after he does the beheading. He's a father of seven and claims that his kids clean his sword at night. I saw the news the day thirty-seven were beheaded and one crucified."

Kady hung her head and slowly uttered words she was ashamed of. "My father watched and was happy to see the infidels get what they deserved. He clapped."

She looked up. "But . . . I am ready to die for Jesus. I've already crossed that bridge in my own mind. I would be honored."

Amina had been listening intently but spoke abruptly. "There's another way, Kady. It doesn't have to end with your death. What if Jesus is calling you to be a missionary sent from Mecca to the rest of the Muslim world? Have you ever thought about that?"

Every person in the room pondered the amazing possibility that Kady might escape Mecca to serve God somewhere else.

Ziad nodded and summarized the group members' thoughts: "Amina, I think the Spirit of God just spoke through you. Amen, sister!"

MIRACLE OF THE EXODUS

In the days following Khaled's appearance at the meeting of the Well, Kady sensed her brothers' attitudes toward her deteriorating. She also felt convinced that Amina's words about Jesus calling her as a missionary sent from Mecca to the rest of the Muslim world were prophetic.

She began a rapid-fire series of clandestine plans, beginning with a request that her mother make an appointment with the family's favorite dentist in Dubai. The trip would be good cover for departing the country. What she didn't know was how urgently her mission trip was needed in order to save her life.

The two brothers planned to use her absence in Dubai to spread the news to the family that they would host the execution of their wayward sister upon her return from the dentist. All she knew was that her friends—and the Spirit of God—were prompting her to go and not come back. To do that, though, she would have to fake her departure to Dubai.

Two days after scheduling her dentist appointment, Khaled and Kady walked together through the north terminal of King Abdulaziz International Airport in Jeddah. Kady pointed to a door.

"Khaled, I have to go to the WC before I get on the plane for Dubai. Be right back!" She tossed a smile at her brother and started to walk away.

"Wait a minute, sister. Not so fast. Give me your phone." Khaled extended his right hand toward the sister he now despised.

Not wanting to create any friction at a critical moment, Kady handed over the phone to her brother and added pleasantly, "Certainly. Here you go."

Once in the designated bathroom stall, Kady heard the whisper she'd hoped for.

"Gate thirty-five."

The woman who quietly delivered the message slipped out of the WC.

Kady pulled off the bright scarf that covered just her hair. Next, she zipped on a full-length, black abaya over her clothes from her carry-on bag. A minute later she emerged from the stall, stuffed her purse, scarf, and bag in the trash can, and slipped her passport into a pocket inside the abaya. She stopped at the mirror to secure the black niqab over her hair and face and prayed that Jesus would go before her.

Good. Only her eyes showed through the niqab. She turned from the mirror and, heart beating wildly, walked out the restroom door.

The Spirit of God brought a scripture to mind: "You keep him in perfect peace whose mind is stayed on you" (ESV). She repeated Isaiah 26:3 to herself several times, and peace flooded her body as she emerged into the airport concourse.

Kady nodded as if in conversation with the women around her who were total strangers. To an observer, she was merely another invisible woman fully shrouded in black. She walked, unrecognized, within an arm's length of Khaled. The brother who was plotting to take her life never even glanced in her direction as she strolled right past him.

At gate 35, Kady hugged Amina, who was waiting with other members of the Well. Her black form shook with emotion as the reality of the dangerous escape from her brother sunk in. Her sisters in Christ, all in abayas and niqabs for cover in case her brother saw them, stood in a circle around Kady. They prayed quietly to Jesus as the line to board the plane inched forward. Kady never glanced back to see if her brother realized he'd been duped. Others were given that assignment. Then, one by one, the escape team stepped to the exit and scanned their boarding passes.

Kady headed down the Jetway and stopped at the doorway of the Airbus A330. She prayed for her Qureshi family, for her new family in the underground church, and for the people of Saudi Arabia. A teary-eyed Kady Qureshi was the last passenger to board Saudi Arabian Airlines Flight 6117 to Beirut.

Face-to-Face

Our escape was timed to the very last minute, so I could get on the flight to Lebanon just before they closed the door of the plane. By the time Khaled realized something was wrong, I was already in the air.

One of our brothers from the Well had gotten special permission to walk the women to the gate. For cover, he dressed in a traditional Saudi dishdasha in case he ran into Khaled.

Walid told us later that as he was leaving the terminal, he heard Khaled screaming at a woman who was cleaning the bathroom. He had run inside the women's restroom, slamming every stall door when he couldn't find me.

We flew out over the Red Sea, which made me think about the Israelites and their escape from Pharaoh in Egypt. God had just done a Red Sea miracle in my life, and even though I was sad to leave everything behind, my heart overflowed with excitement at the thought of being a missionary to Muslims.

My father left a message for me on Amina's phone saying that the whole family was gathered at a birthday party for one of our cousins, that they missed me, and that they wanted me to come back. But I knew the real reason they were gathered. They had come together to execute me because of my love for Jesus. My brothers had it all planned.

How sick is that?

But Jesus had other plans for me!

So much has happened since my escape from Mecca. The Well had to go deeper underground and relocate outside the city, but there are other churches still meeting in Mecca. Everyone survived, though, and is faithfully serving the Lord in Saudi Arabia.

Khaled and Wahhab went manic in their search for me. Eventually they figured out I was in Lebanon. One day on a walk in Beirut with some Lebanese believers, I actually spotted them at a distance and ducked into a building. I watched until they were out of sight.

Despite my brothers' seething anger, I felt God's presence and His perfect peace. After the close encounter in Beirut, though, I knew it was just a matter of time before they found me. So I left Lebanon for the West.

Because of the many refugees and immigrants from Muslim areas coming to Western countries, this is an unprecedented time to reach out to them with the love of Christ. Muslims who settle in new places often feel unwanted, unloved, and overlooked. I can certainly relate to those feelings.

As a Muslim woman, I felt the same way Amina did before Jesus rescued her. I felt invisible at times. But El Roi— the God who sees—saw me and saved me.

And I can tell you that where you live, Muslims— especially women—want to be seen. They feel invisible, especially if they've been wearing Islamic coverings.

Our ministry friends in the West often say, "The Muslims are coming, the Muslims are coming . . . the Muslims are here! So what are we going to do about it?"

Jesus brought them to the cities we live in, and it's a great opportunity to see Muslims come to faith in Christ.

Reach out to them by simply starting a conversation. That will lead to a friendship that leads to sharing the amazing words of life Jesus offers.

Let's reach them together for Jesus! Would you join me in praying that millions of Muslims would give their lives to Jesus, and that many of my people in Saudi Arabia would too? I would also be very grateful if you would pray specifically for my family.

From Mecca, Saudi Arabia, where the religion of Islam began fourteen hundred years ago, I truly am privileged to be a missionary for Jesus to Muslims. And the Muslims I'm called to reach in serving Jesus Christ? I'm amazed that my mission field is . . . *the USA.*

But the Lord stood by me and strengthened me, so that through me the message might be fully proclaimed and all Gentiles might hear it. So I was rescued from the lion's mouth.

—2 TIMOTHY 4:17 ESV

NOW THAT I'M INSPIRED, WHAT DO I DO?

America has sent more missionaries for Christ to the world than any other nation in history. But in our last chapter, "The Great Mecca Escape," we introduced a former Muslim from Mecca who has come to America to reach Muslims for Christ.

How's that for an unexpected turn of events!

Missionaries coming to America?

That's right, and there are many of them. Kady is part of the new generation of Muslim-background believers who are passionate about following Jesus and making His name known, no matter the cost.

WHAT WE'VE LEARNED

There are three important lessons we've taken away from the experiences of the courageous women whose stories we've shared:

1. Danger Is Temporary

   Dina from "The Worst Marriage in Syria" is laser focused on reaching Muslim women in refugee camps filled with Islamic fundamentalists. The probability that one day she will die doing this has little bearing on her life. Her faith overrides the normal human reaction to flee from danger.

   We talk about keeping our eyes on Jesus, but Dina lives this out in situations that would make an armed soldier run for cover. That's why she says, "All of life is temporary. It's eternity that counts." Dina teaches us to put danger in perspective. It's not forever. Another friend in the Middle East says, "It's not a time for sissy Christians." We get the point.

2. Pray for Miracles and Expect Them

   In the West we often hear Christians ask the question, "Do you think God still does miracles?" Can you imagine what God thinks when He hears His children discussing things like this? The women and men in this book would never ask that question because the Bible says God does miracles.

   Dina and Mohammad tell us to *expect* miracles. Jamila, who defied a death sentence, saw her entire family come to faith in Christ—and they were fundamentalist Muslims. These believers teach us that wishy-washy prayers don't get answered. We should pray in faith and expect miracles.

3. Prayer Is for the Long Haul

The women in this book are prayer *warriors*. Hearing them pray would change how you pray. They know prayer is not always accompanied by immediate results. But God calls us to always be faithful and abounding in prayer.

In some cases, God calls us to pray for years. One of the reasons that the women in this book stay where they live and embrace the chaos around them is not just to share the gospel with others. It's also to soak the people in prayer. Sometimes answers come after *months* of prayer turn into *years* of prayer.

I (JoAnn) often share Micah 7:7–8. These are beautiful verses, full of hope that God intends for you to rest in:

> But as for me, I *watch* in hope for the Lord,
> I *wait* for God my Savior;
> my God will hear me.

> Do not gloat over me, my enemy!
> Though I have fallen, I will rise.
> Though I sit in darkness,
> the Lord will be my light. (emphasis added)

Prayer is like a rocking chair. Sitting in one, you rock back and forth as you talk to the Father about the concerns of your heart. First, you rock forward, gazing right to left, asking yourself and the Lord, "Is this the day of Your answer?" You're *watching* for His divine provision. When you don't see the answer coming, you rock back, *waiting* for His perfect timing. Your hope is firmly established on His promise that He hears you. You continue rocking forward and backward, you're continually renewed in His presence, as you *watch* expectantly for His answer, then rest again, *waiting* while He works. And one day, as you *watch* in hope, Jesus will fulfill the desire of your heart in ways that your mind cannot conceive (1 Cor. 2:9).

THE HARSH REALITY

The three lessons we've learned—danger is temporary, pray for miracles and expect them, and prayer is for the long haul—are essentials for these women of God because of the reality that they live with every day.

At the beginning of this book, we said that in 1979, the United Nations adopted an international treaty concerning the overall treatment of women. The Convention on the Elimination of All Forms of Discrimination Against Women, or CEDAW, is now more than forty years old.

CEDAW has been called the international bill of rights for women, and the overall goal is to eliminate prejudices and customs based on the idea that women are inferior to men. The treaty also seeks to suppress all forms of sex trafficking, prostitution, and violence and to give women the freedom to enter marriage with a spouse they freely choose.

But in December 2019, some Palestinian clans in the West

Bank rejected this treaty even though it was implemented four decades ago. They claimed that the provisions of the treaty *were not compatible with the religion of Islam.*

Sadly, these clans are not alone in their thinking. In fundamentalist Muslim areas, their way is the "old normal." Men rule, control, and dominate women, and it begins with the first male relationship they have in life: *with their own fathers.*

The Devil has had it in for women since the garden of Eden when Adam and Eve fell into sin. God judged Satan because he deceived Eve. And that began Satan's ongoing war with women, to get even. One of his attacks is to deceive women into believing they don't deserve the love of their fathers, and, in turn, they aren't worthy of a heavenly Father's love. But nothing could be further from the truth. Strict Islam reinforces this thinking and inevitably leads women into crushing spiritual bondage.

So it's easy to see why Muslim women who have experienced male rule, control, and domination in their lives assume that's what God must be like.

THE RESCUE OPERATION

No wonder Jesus is rescuing women in the Muslim world. His heart goes out to them. For the first time in their lives, women who have been raised in a culture that is unfair and demeaning to them are treated with respect, compassion, fairness, and love. They experience all this in a relationship with the God of heaven, their loving *Father.*

Who wouldn't want that?

The women you met in *Women Who Risk* emerged from painful, unyielding situations in which men had all the rights and privileges, and they were left with little in life.

All of that changed when they met Jesus. Boy did it ever!

Each of these women eagerly responded to His message once they learned the truth about Him. When they confessed their sins and embraced Jesus Christ as Savior, they began a new life that came chock-full of eternal rewards. They are now daughters of the King of kings.

But the majority of people they live around don't see Jesus as the King of kings. To them, He's merely a prophet. The fact that Jesus means everything to believers is seen as an all-out defection from the Islamic faith, their family, and their heritage.

The future, though, is glorious even while their present is a life of extreme danger.

The danger was a nonfactor in their decision—a minor detail. These are, after all, women who risk. They are women ready to die for Jesus. Meanwhile, He has called them to a special mission to reach the Muslim world.

Because of the religious and cultural norms for women in Islamic areas, who would ever expect them to be major players in the growing underground church? They're secret agents for the Lord because they're the spiritual gatekeepers of their families. That's where their work begins, and they move out from there.

The religion of Islam has captured one-fifth of planet Earth's population, and today Muslim refugees and immigrants are dispersing around the globe. As we've said before, *the Muslims are coming, the Muslims are coming . . . the Muslims are here!*

WHERE YOU COME IN

We're hopeful that through these stories of women who have risked everything, including their own lives, you've seen that Muslims are turning to Jesus. What does that mean for the rest of us? God calls us to live out our faith and to be salt and light for Him. In that, you may wonder what it is you can do. This is where we suggest you begin:

1. Push Through the Fear!

   Why do women living in danger willingly risk their lives for Jesus? It's because, for the first time in their lives, these once-forgotten women have received love and freedom, and now they are not ashamed of the gospel of Christ. They've seen the truth of Romans 1:16 in action.

   When sharing the good news of Jesus Christ, the power of God is released for salvation for those who believe. They long for others to "taste and see that the LORD is good" (Ps. 34:8). We, too, can embrace this biblical principle by never being ashamed to tell others about Jesus—including Muslims who are searching for the Truth. To push through the fear, you'll have to stop getting your worldview from the news and start seeing Muslims as human beings just like anyone else.

   Is there a global problem with Islamic terrorism? Of course there is. But the majority of Muslims are *not* terrorists. Jesus said the gospel is for all people, that He would build His church, and that it would burst through the gates of hell (Matt. 16:18). He's blowing the gates of Islam wide open, just as He said He would. So push through your fear. Jesus is leading us through the open gates.

2. Pray for Muslims as If It's Their Last Day on Earth

It was once said, "Prayer is the slender vein that moves the hand of God." But we often don't pray because we aren't desperate enough to pray *urgently*. But would you pray differently if you knew there was no tomorrow?

The women you met in the pages of this book exemplify the power of intercession. They saw the spiritual mountains in their lives thrown into the sea as they persisted in critical prayer. We must do the same.

Pray for Muslims to come to Christ as you drive by a mosque. When you see a veiled woman, pray that Jesus will meet her in her dreams, setting her on a mission to find out who He really is. Pray for more boldness to share your faith with others, including Muslims.

3. Practice Compassion, and Cool It with the Condemning

According to John 3:17, "God did not send his Son into the world to condemn the world, but to save the world through him." During His earthly ministry, Jesus poured life into people, and His heart was to see their eternity altered and their souls saved.

If we follow the example of Jesus, our mission on planet Earth is not to condemn Muslims but to love them. Compassion is birthed when our eyes focus on this perspective.

When you see a Muslim woman (many stand out in their hijabs), show them you see them and make pleasant conversation with them. They have falsely believed that they don't matter, so when we pretend that we don't see them or ignore them, we reinforce the lie the Devil has convinced them is true. As you make friends with Muslims and follow the previous two suggestions, you could just be the blessed one to lead them to faith in Jesus.

WANT TO GET MORE INVOLVED?

Because every soul matters, here are four ways to make a difference. It takes just one visit to https://unchartedministries.com, and you can

1. receive monthly updates and pray for the women on the front lines,
2. support women on the front lines through **Not Forgotten**, which is the women's division of **Uncharted Ministries**,
3. schedule a "Seen" gathering with JoAnn and the **Not Forgotten** team at your church or women's Bible study (**Not Forgotten** has trained thousands of believers to reach Muslim women in America, Europe, South America, Asia, and, of course, the Middle East. Our team has a goal of establishing a lighthouse for Muslim women in all fifty states in North America and in every European country. Want to make a difference? Schedule a gathering.), and
4. watch inspiring videos of Muslim-background believers

(MBBs) who have risked it all to follow Jesus. (You can meet them at "I Found the Truth" on the **Uncharted** website.)

THE GREAT COMMISSION INCLUDES MUSLIMS!

It's been our joy to introduce you to our friends in the Middle East, the *women who risk*. These spiritual gatekeepers are a key to God's work. Reach a Muslim woman, and you reach the Muslim world.

Since they are all former Muslims and because most remain right in the heart of Islam, out of necessity they live like secret agents for Jesus. In fact, as we were writing these final words today, one of our **Uncharted Ministries'** underground women's Bible studies was discovered. It's the Bible study that I (JoAnn) met with in chapter 5. The women meet in a Muslim fundamentalist area, and the Islamic State sent a handwritten note promising to kill all whom they suspect are now followers of Christ. Yep, ISIS is still around. Their hunch was right. These former Muslim women are all now believers in Christ. How privileged we are to have just written their stories. Please pray for them.

But despite the threat, they are not in the least bit deterred. They just changed the location of the Bible study.

In the West we don't have the same kinds of challenges, but we need wisdom in relating to Muslims who move into our cities and neighborhoods. Plus, we need God's heart to move us to action.

The Muslims are coming, the Muslims are coming . . . the Muslims are here!

With our sisters on the front lines of the battle, let's join together to reach Muslims for Christ and for the glory of God!

ACKNOWLEDGMENTS

O ur highest praise goes to Jesus! For Your name and renown is the desire of our hearts!

To the women whose stories are told in *Women Who Risk*: The thrilling accounts of how Jesus rescued you and how you now serve Him fearlessly have changed our lives. We love you.

Utmost love and honor to our fabulous family: Since our head count officially hit twenty-three—with our six children, the married-ins, and our eleven grandchildren (and counting), we'll hold back from naming each one of you.

Thank you for cheering Dad (Poppy) and Mom (Noni) on. Your words of encouragement, high fives, and understanding when we missed various family gatherings have made this exciting project a little lighter. We're so proud of the men and women of God you are and the godly ways you're raising your children. Doing life with you is the greatest highlight and treasure of our lives.

Thank you, Mom Renda, or Gigi, as all the grands and great-grands call you: you model Jesus to us with your passion for Him combined with your heart of serving and sharing Jesus with everyone you meet.

Profound gratitude to our awesome trailblazing colleagues in the spiritual trenches who make up our **Uncharted** team: Tommy, Josh and Jessie, Bruce, Gina, Kathleen, Angel, Candy, Jessica, Laura, Lisa, Sharon, Jeff, and Pat and Cheri.

We have cherished traveling the **Uncharted** world with you, sharing the light and love of Jesus with the **Not Forgotten** message. How indebted we are to the **Uncharted** national leaders throughout the Middle East. How we are inspired by you and your willingness to suffer and die for Jesus. Each of you has a "foot-washing spirit" that reminds us of Jesus. Thank you for walking alongside us.

Deep appreciation and thanks to the stellar W Publishing Group, especially Debbie Wickwire, Damon Reiss, Paula Major, Alex Woods, and Whitney Bak. Thank you for recognizing the importance of platforming the mighty works of God currently happening in the Muslim world. Your polish and input have been timeless, as well as your friendship.

Greg Webster, we are grateful for your creative juices and attention to detail. Thank you for seeing our hearts and helping us capture these amazing God-stories for His glory. Cheers to completing our fourth project together.

Thank you, David Shepherd, for believing in us and launching us into the exciting world of writing. We couldn't have done this without you.

Because every soul matters to Jesus, you matter to us.

NOTES

PREFACE

1. Khaled Abu Toameh, "Palestinian Clans Reject Treaty Ending Discrimination Against Women," *Jerusalem Post*, December 23, 2019, https://www.jpost.com/Middle-East/Palestinian-clans -reject-treaty-ending-discrimination-against-women-611811.

CHAPTER 1: DELIVER US FROM EVIL

1. *Jinns* is an ancient Arabic reference to supernatural spirits. In this context, demons.
2. *Jummah* is Islam's Friday prayer practice. Every Friday Muslims gather for congregational prayer, or Jummah, the most important prayer of the week.
3. *Marhaba* is an Arabic greeting that means "Welcome" or "Hello."
4. Abdullah Yusuf Ali, trans., *The Holy Qur'an: English Translation and Commentary* (Indianapolis: American Trust Publications for the Muslim Student's Association of the United States and Canada, 1977).

CHAPTER 2: THE WORST MARRIAGE IN SYRIA

1. "Ancient City of Aleppo," UNESCO World Heritage Centre, accessed May 7, 2020, https://whc.unesco.org/en/list/21/.
2. "Ten Oldest Cities in the World," EducationWorld, accessed June 17, 2020, https://www.educationworld.in/10-oldest-cities-in-the-world/.
3. Iain Overton and Jennifer Dathan, "Syria in 2020: The Deadly Legacy of Explosive Violence and Its Impact on Infrastructure and Health," ReliefWeb, December 18, 2019, https://reliefweb .int/report/syrian-arab-republic/syria-2020-deadly-legacy -explosive-violence-and-its-impact.
4. *Basbousa* is a popular Middle Eastern sweet cake.
5. A *mut'ah* is a contract for a temporary "pleasure marriage" approved by a sheikh or imam.
6. Karin Laub, "Aleppo Confronts Vast Destruction Left by 4 Years of War," Associated Press, December 22, 2016, https:// www.apnews.com/00640d3a1566472cb7c176aadb065f81.
7. *As-salaam-alaikum* is an Arabic greeting meaning "Peace be to you."

CHAPTER 3: "MARRY HIM, OR YOUR MOTHER DIES!"

1. Michael Jansen, "Jordan Economy Groans Under the Weight of Refugee Crisis," *Irish Times*, October 19, 2018, https://www .irishtimes.com/news/world/middle-east/jordan-economy -groans-under-the-weight-of-refugee-crisis-1.3669366.
2. The acronym UNRWA stands for "United Nations Relief and Works Agency."
3. In US currency the value of Jordanian dinars or JDs, also known as JODs, is almost $3,000.
4. *Baba* is an Arabic term of endearment for a father, similar to "Daddy" or "Papa."
5. *Abayas* are full-length, loose outer garments worn by many Muslim women.

CHAPTER 4: THE LIAR FROM LEBANON

1. Marmaduke William Pickthall, trans., *Al-Qur'an Al-Karim* (Islamabad, Pakistan: Islamic Research Institute, 1988).
2. *Habibi* is an Arabic term of affection for a friend, significant other, or family member, literally meaning "my love," "my dear," "my darling," or "beloved."
3. Anything that is forbidden for Muslims is *haram*.

CHAPTER 5: HOPELESS—THEN JESUS ARRIVED

1. A *muezzin* is the person at a mosque designated to offer the call to prayer.

CHAPTER 6: TRAPPED IN GAZA

1. Judah Ari Gross, "2 More Israelis Killed by Gaza Fire; IDF Assassinates Hamas Moneyman," *The Times of Israel*, May 5, 2019, https://www.timesofisrael.com/2-more-israelis-killed-by -gaza-fire-idf-assassinates-hamas-moneyman/.
2. Ibid.
3. Ibid.
4. Brouria Bitton-Ashkelony and Aryeh Kofsky, eds., *Christian Gaza in Late Antiquity* (Leiden, Netherlands: Brill, 2004), 68–69. See also Entsar Abu Jahal, "Ancient Gaza Monastery Gets Second Life as Children's Library," Al-Monitor, June 1, 2016, https:// www.al-monitor.com/pulse/originals/2016/06/restoration -khodr-shrine-monastary-gaza-library-children.html.
5. *Shukran* is Arabic for "Thank you."
6. Anna Ahronheim, "Shin Bet Arrests Hamas Explosive Expert in Israel with Humanitarian Permit," *Jerusalem Post*, July 3, 2019, https://www.jpost.com/israel-news/shin-bet-arrests-hamas -explosive-expert-in-israel-with-humanitarian-permit-594474.

CHAPTER 7: THE GREAT MECCA ESCAPE

1. *Al-Masjid al-Haram* is the Great Mosque of Mecca, built at the site of Muhammad's birth.

2. The *hajj* is the annual Islamic pilgrimage to Mecca, Saudi Arabia.

3. The *Kaaba* is a small building in the court of the Great Mosque that houses a sacred Muslim stone relic. This is the holiest place for Muslims in the world.

4. A *mutawa* is an enforcer of Islamic religious law.

5. *Sabah alkhyr* is Arabic for "Good morning."

ABOUT THE AUTHORS

Tom Doyle is the president of **Uncharted Ministries**, an accomplished author, popular international speaker, pastor, missionary to the unreached, and a veteran tour guide in Israel and the Middle East. He is the author of *Dreams and Visions*, *Killing Christians*, and *Standing in the Fire*. Tom graduated from Biola University and Dallas Theological Seminary.

JoAnn Doyle is the founder of **Not Forgotten**, the women's ministry division of **Uncharted Ministries**, and a popular international speaker, voice for women in the Middle East, and missionary. She leads women's ministry teams into Israel and also the heart of the Muslim world.

Greg Webster is cofounder of New Vantage Publishing Partners and creative director of Webster Creative Group.

ABOUT THE AUTHORS

The collaborator of more than a dozen books for a variety of authors, he holds an MA in theology from Fuller Theological Seminary and a BA in journalism and an MBA from the University of Georgia.

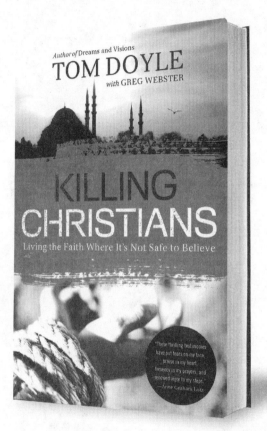

also from
TOM DOYLE

Middle Eastern heroes of faith who fear God more than terrorist groups such as ISIS—real-life stories from Tom Doyle that reveal how these Christians are living not as victims but as victors in Christ.